P9-CUK-094

DATE DUE

DEC 1 7 2013			

Demco, Inc. 38-293

1st EDITION

Perspectives on Diseases and Disorders

Attention Deficit Hyperactivity Disorder

Jacqueline Langwith
Book Editor

PERSPECTIVES
On Diseases & Disorders

LIBRARY
Milwaukee Area
Technical College
WEST CAMPUS

616.8589
P467

g™

Detroit • New York • San Francisco • New Haven, Conn • Waterville, Maine • London

GALE
CENGAGE Learning™

Christine Nasso, *Publisher*
Elizabeth Des Chenes, *Managing Editor*

© 2009 Greenhaven Press, a part of Gale, Cengage Learning

Gale and Greenhaven Press are registered trademarks used herein under license.

For more information, contact:
Greenhaven Press
27500 Drake Rd.
Farmington Hills, MI 48331-3535
Or you can visit our Internet site at gale.cengage.com

ALL RIGHTS RESERVED.
No part of this work covered by the copyright herein may be reproduced, transmitted, stored, or used in any form or by any means graphic, electronic, or mechanical, including but not limited to photocopying, recording, scanning, digitizing, taping, Web distribution, information networks, or information storage and retrieval systems, except as permitted under Section 107 or 108 of the 1976 United States Copyright Act, without the prior written permission of the publisher.

For product information and technology assistance, contact us at

Gale Customer Support, 1-800-877-4253
For permission to use material from this text or product, submit all requests online at www.cengage.com/permissions

Further permissions questions can be emailed to permissionrequest@cengage.com

Articles in Greenhaven Press anthologies are often edited for length to meet page requirements. In addition, original titles of these works are changed to clearly present the main thesis and to explicitly indicate the author's opinion. Every effort is made to ensure that Greenhaven Press accurately reflects the original intent of the authors. Every effort has been made to trace the owners of copyrighted material.

Cover image Joe Raedle/Getty Images

LIBRARY OF CONGRESS CATALOGING-IN-PUBLICATION DATA

Attention deficit hyperactivity disorder / Jacqueline Langwith, book editor.
    p. cm. -- (Perspectives on diseases and disorders)
  Includes bibliographical references and index.
  ISBN 978-0-7377-4378-4 (hardcover)
  1. Attention-deficit hyperactivity disorder. I. Langwith, Jacqueline.
  RJ506.H9A925 2009
  618.92'8589--dc22

                                                    2009003288

Printed in the United States of America
  2 3 4 5 6 7 13 12 11 10 09

CONTENTS

Foreword   7

Introduction   9

CHAPTER 1   Understanding ADHD

1. The Characteristics of Attention   16
   Deficit Hyperactivity Disorder
   Paula Anne Ford-Martin, Teresa G. Odle,
   and Helen Davidson
   ADHD is a developmental disorder characterized
   by distractibility, hyperactivity, and an inability
   to focus.

2. Many Adults Have ADHD   26
   Diana Mahoney
   A significant number of adults have attention
   deficit hyperactivity disorder, and many are not
   getting the treatment they need.

3. Girls Also Suffer from ADHD   33
   Nicole Crawford
   Although statistics indicate that ADHD primarily
   affects boys, many girls also have the condition,
   and scientists are trying to learn more about
   how ADHD affects females.

4. ADHD Is Related to Delayed Brain Growth   41
   Lindsay Minnema
   A study provides biological evidence that ADHD
   is due to delayed growth in a certain part of the
   brain.

5. ADHD Genes May Have Been Helpful   **46**
for Ancient Nomads

William Saletan

Symptoms of ADHD, such as hyperactivity, impulsivity, and distractibility, may have been helpful for nomadic tribes.

6. Brain Imaging May Help Diagnose and   **51**
Treat ADHD

Claire Shipman and Ariane Nalty

Brain tests can reveal details about brain functioning that help doctors diagnose ADHD and prescribe the most effective treatment for it.

CHAPTER 2   Controversies About ADHD

1. ADHD Is a Real Medical Disorder   **59**

Stephen V. Faraone

ADHD meets the six criteria that medicine uses to determine the validity of psychiatric diagnoses.

2. ADHD Is Not a Real Medical Disorder   **67**

Sami Timimi and Nick Radcliffe

ADHD is not a medical disorder. It is a cultural phenomenon created by society and a diagnosis that can actually harm children.

3. ADHD Is Underdiagnosed and Undertreated   **77**

William Dodson

Studies show that ADHD is more common than prevalence rates suggest and that many people diagnosed with ADHD are not being treated.

4. ADHD Is Overdiagnosed and ADHD 89
Medications Are Overprescribed

Tom Glaister

There is a disturbing trend in America of labeling kids with ADHD and then pressuring their parents to give them psychostimulant drugs.

5. Alternative Therapies May Be Useful in 98
Treating ADHD

Tara Parker-Pope

Concerns about the side effects of ADHD drugs are causing many people to consider alternative treatments.

6. Children Should Undergo Heart Screening 103
Before Taking Stimulants to Treat ADHD

D. Woodrow Benson and Christena H. Benson

Ordering electrocardiograms to screen children for heart problems before prescribing stimulants to treat ADHD can be useful.

7. Children Do Not Need to Undergo Heart 109
Screening Before Taking Stimulants to
Treat ADHD

Lawrence Diller

Electrocardiograms for children with ADHD are not necessary because the risk of sudden cardiac death from ADHD drugs is infinitesimally small.

CHAPTER 3   Personal Experiences with ADHD

1. My Life Changed for the Better After My 116
ADHD Diagnosis and Treatment

Ann Barkin, as told to Sandy Fertman Ryan

A teenager describes how finding out she has ADHD and receiving treatment helped her make positive changes in her life.

2. Living with the Tics That Accompany My ADHD   121

Blake E.S. Taylor

A young man with ADHD talks about tics, one of the common disorders that can accompany ADHD.

3. My Son's Story   127

Laurie Hagberg

A teacher talks about the lessons she has learned through her own son's struggles with ADHD.

Glossary   134

Chronology   140

Organizations to Contact   143

For Further Reading   147

Index   151

FOREWORD

"Medicine, to produce health, has to examine disease."
—Plutarch

Independent research on a health issue is often the first step to complement discussions with a physician. But locating accurate, well-organized, understandable medical information can be a challenge. A simple Internet search on terms such as "cancer" or "diabetes," for example, returns an intimidating number of results. Sifting through the results can be daunting, particularly when some of the information is inconsistent or even contradictory. The Greenhaven Press series Perspectives on Diseases and Disorders offers a solution to the often overwhelming nature of researching diseases and disorders.

From the clinical to the personal, titles in the Perspectives on Diseases and Disorders series provide student and other researchers with authoritative, accessible information in unique anthologies that include basic information about the disease or disorder, controversial aspects of diagnosis and treatment, and first-person accounts of those impacted by the disease. The result is a well-rounded combination of primary and secondary sources that, together, provide the reader with a better understanding of the disease or disorder.

Each volume in Perspectives on Diseases and Disorders explores a particular disease or disorder in detail. Material for each volume is carefully selected from a wide range of sources, including encyclopedias, journals, newspapers, nonfiction books, speeches, government documents, pamphlets, organization newsletters, and position papers. Articles in the first chapter provide an authoritative, up-to-date overview that covers symptoms, causes and effects, treatments, cures, and medical advances. The second chapter presents a substantial number of opposing viewpoints on controversial treatments and other current debates relating to the volume topic. The third chapter offers a variety of personal perspectives on the disease or disorder. Patients, doctors, caregivers, and loved ones represent just some of the voices found in this narrative chapter.

Each Perspectives on Diseases and Disorders volume also includes:

- An **annotated table of contents** that provides a brief summary of each article in the volume.
- An **introduction** specific to the volume topic.
- Full-color **charts and graphs** to illustrate key points, concepts, and theories.
- Full-color **photos** that show aspects of the disease or disorder and enhance textual material.
- **"Fast Facts"** that highlight pertinent additional statistics and surprising points.
- A **glossary** providing users with definitions of important terms.
- A **chronology** of important dates relating to the disease or disorder.
- An annotated list of **organizations to contact** for students and other readers seeking additional information.
- A **bibliography** of additional books and periodicals for further research.
- A detailed **subject index** that allows readers to quickly find the information they need.

Whether a student researching a disorder, a patient recently diagnosed with a disease, or an individual who simply wants to learn more about a particular disease or disorder, a reader who turns to Perspectives on Diseases and Disorders will find a wealth of information in each volume that offers not only basic information, but also vigorous debate from multiple perspectives.

INTRODUCTION

J eff, a nineteen-year-old college student at Columbia University, has just "scored" some Adderall, an amphetamine-based drug used to treat attention deficit hyperactivity disorder (ADHD). It is 10:00 P.M. and he's tired—he's been awake since his early morning English class, and he worked the evening shift as a waiter at a local restaurant. But Jeff has an important physics test tomorrow, and he needs to do well. The Adderall will help keep him awake and focused so he can study. Jeff obtained the Adderall from one of his college buddies who has a prescription for it. His friend has plenty of Adderall and does not mind giving a few pills to Jeff, especially if it is going to help him study and do well on a test.

While this situation is hypothetical, studies show that students at colleges throughout the United States are improperly using ADHD medications, typically obtained from their friends who have ADHD. Various groups of people have concerns about this. Health professionals are worried about the side effects of ADHD medications and the potential for drug addiction. Some students are upset because they think using these medications as "study aids" is a form of cheating, and students with ADHD who really need Adderall or Ritalin generally have mixed feelings.

A growing number of time-frazzled college students are turning to ADHD medications to help them study. Although it seems counterintuitive, stimulants like Adderall and Ritalin are the most common treatment to help those with ADHD relax and focus. For most people without ADHD, however, stimulants "arouse" the nervous system and increase awareness and alertness. Adderall and Ritalin are favorites of busy college students

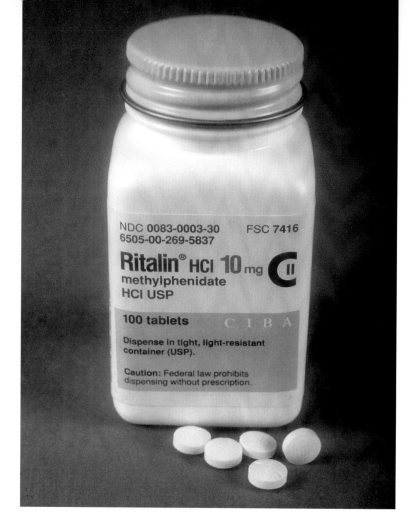

A survey of college students indicates that ADHD medications are commonly misused. (Yvonne Hemsey/Getty Images)

because the medications keep them alert and focused through all-night study sessions. Students say ADHD medications make studying more interesting, and the drugs actually make them *want* to study. "I take Adderall anytime that I need to be studying for a long period of time," Florida State University junior Jenn Kapatkin said in an article in the school's newspaper, the *Florida Flambeau*. "I need it to focus. I found that the more you take it, the less it works, so I only take it when I need it. It makes me want to sit down and study and concentrate on what I need to. I don't get easily distracted by other things when I'm on Adderall," said Kapatkin.

A broad survey of college students indicates that ADHD medications are commonly misused. In 2007 the results of a survey of nearly eleven thousand students from 119 universities across the country were released. More than 4 percent of the students surveyed reported that they had used a stimulant, such as Adderall or Ritalin, without a prescription during the previous year. At some schools as much as 25 percent of the student body reported past-year use of one of these stimulants. The survey results indicate that the typical nonprescription user of ADHD medications is a white male fraternity member at an elite northeastern college. Not surprisingly, Adderall is often called "ivy-league crack," in reference to crack cocaine, a devastating and highly addictive drug used primarily by urban African Americans in the 1980s.

Health professionals are concerned about college students' misuse of ADHD medications. Both Adderall, an amphetamine, and Ritalin, a close relative of cocaine, are Schedule II controlled substances. They have high potential for abuse, are potentially very addictive, and their use and distribution are illegal without a prescription. According to Ellen Trappey, a substance abuse and prevention specialist at St. Joseph's University in Philadelphia, students underestimate the dangers of taking Adderall without a prescription. Says Trappey, "I don't think that many students understand the effect Adderall has on a person's body, especially if the person taking it has not seen a doctor and is not prescribed the medication." Common side effects of stimulants like Adderall and Ritalin include weight loss, the inability to fall asleep or stay asleep, abnormal heartbeats, abdominal pain, and abnormal muscle movements and twitching. More serious risks include psychosis and cardiac arrest. The U.S. Food and Drug Administration requires that prescriptions of Adderall and Ritalin include a "black box" label warning that the drugs may lead to an increased risk of sudden cardiac death. However, students who obtain a few pills from a friend probably do not see the warning. Richard Sogn, a psychiatrist from Portland, Oregon, and a contributor to *WebMD.com*, is concerned about the addictive nature of Adderall. He says, "People who use amphetamines for the 'high,' to increase wakefulness and increase stamina, or to decrease appetite, often continue to use these drugs, often need higher and higher doses to achieve the same effects, and develop a drug problem." Health professionals worry that college students are not considering the risks when they pop a few Adderall or Ritalin capsules to help them do well on a test.

The majority of college students who misuse ADHD medications do not think they are doing anything wrong. A number of factors contribute to this view. First, college students and young people in general tend to think they are "immortal" and unlikely to come to any harm. Second, many students mistakenly think that Adderall and Ritalin must be safe since they are prescription drugs. They think that if it is safe for their friend who has ADHD, then it must be safe for them. Finally, students think that anything that helps their grade point average cannot be bad. The mentality is that since it is used for academic purposes rather than recreational purposes, it is OK. In a story in the University of Maryland's newspaper, the *Diamondback*, a student named Catherine says the following about using Ritalin or Adderall without a prescription: "As many negative effects as there are, the positives are so much better—you perform well at school and stay on task all throughout the day." Keene State College student Julie Emmond questions whether using Adderall or Ritalin is that much different than downing an energy drink or a cup of coffee. Writing in Keene's *Equinox*, she says:

> Many people drink coffee or use energy drinks to keep them focused and other people drink so much caffeine that they can't function without it. Similarly, some people find that certain doses of ADHD drugs help them get a lot of school work done from time to time. So is the use of ADHD medication without a prescription really that different from other legal stimulant use?

College students who actually have ADHD have mixed feelings about the popularity of the medications they need. Many college students who were diagnosed with ADHD as children have refillable prescriptions for Adderall or Ritalin. However, they do not always take their medications, and their excess pills are the biggest source of these drugs for other students on campus. In an article in the *New York Times*, Columbia University student Libby, who was diagnosed with ADHD in the first grade, says she only takes her medication when she has to write a big paper. That leaves her with lots of extra pills, which she sells to strangers or trades with friends for meals. According to Libby, the demand for "study buddies"—as Adderall and Ritalin are often called—can get intense during exam weeks. "I'm constantly being bombarded with requests," she says. Libby doesn't think there is anything wrong with selling her extra pills. She has even found a greater acceptance toward taking ADHD medications. She says when she was a kid she used to feel "different" for taking Ritalin. Now, however, "it's almost cool to take them," she says. Other students with ADHD, however, are not happy that Ritalin and Adderall are "cool." In an article in the University of Pennsylvania's *Daily Pennsylvanian*, a student named John says that he has to jump through hoops to renew his Ritalin prescription, which he badly needs. He says, "Every time I need a new prescription, I have to go into the doctor's office and pay a fee. The doctors are suspicious because so many kids fake needing it," he says.

Doctors say it is sometimes hard to sort out those with a legitimate ADHD diagnosis from those who are faking it. Many students get Adderall and Ritalin by going to their family doctor or to the college health clinic and feigning the symptoms of ADHD. In an article in *The Yale Daily News*, a student named Eleanor says she occasionally uses Adderall obtained from a doctor. According to Eleanor, "If you want it and you're tactful and persistent, you can get it." In a 2004 study, introductory psychology students at the University of California's Los Angeles campus were given one of four commonly used diagnostic tests for ADHD and were asked to answer as if they were afflicted with the disorder. The students were easily able to trick all four of the diagnostic tests. Doctors may try to identify the fakers by making the diagnostic process more in-depth, such as by interviewing other people in the student's life. However, they must be cognizant of the fact that some students do have undiagnosed ADHD that is just being discovered in their college years.

Some college students who do not use ADHD medications believe that using them without a prescription is tantamount to academic cheating. In a *New York Times* article, Columbia student Angelica Gonzales says all of her friends have taken Adderall at some point in their college careers, and she is resentful. She says, "It's cheating, and it really bothers me. I mean, everyone here is smart. They should be able to get by without the extra help." Santa Clara University student Chris Cavagnero agrees. He says using Adderall for studying is analogous to steroid use in baseball. "Steroid users are cheaters because they use an illicit substance to gain an unfair advantage over the competition." But not everyone agrees. University of Arizona student David Schultz believes taking Adderall or Ritalin for studying is "no more advantageous than slamming a few six packs of Red Bull." Schultz, who doesn't use either medication, goes on to say, "Take all the pills you want. I am confident in putting my work up against that of the jittery, tweaked-out guy sitting next to me who has yet to notice the scalding hot coffee he's spilled on his own shaky hand."

CHAPTER 1

Understanding ADHD

The Characteristics of Attention Deficit Hyperactivity Disorder

Paula Anne Ford-Martin, Teresa G. Odle, and Helen Davidson

In the following selection Paula Anne Ford-Martin, Teresa G. Odle, and Helen Davidson discuss the causes, symptoms, diagnosis, and treatment of attention deficit hyperactivity disorder (ADHD). According to the authors, ADHD is a developmental disorder causing distractibility, hyperactivity, and impulsive behaviors. The authors say that the exact cause of ADHD is not known, but several factors seem to be important: genetics, prenatal exposure to toxins or poor nutrition, and traumatic brain injury may all trigger ADHD. According to the authors, about half of all children afflicted with ADHD will outgrow the disease. Paula Anne Ford-Martin, Teresa G. Odle, and Helen Davidson are nationally published medical writers.

A ttention-deficit/hyperactivity disorder (ADHD) is a developmental disorder characterized by distractibility, hyperactivity, impulsive behaviors,

Photo on previous page. ADHD is a developmental disorder causing distractibility, hyperactivity, and impulsive behavior. (Image copyright Junial Enterprises, 2009. Used under license from Shutterstock.com.)

SOURCE: Paula Anne Ford-Martin, Teresa G. Odle, and Helen Davidson, "Attention Deficit/Hyperactivity Disorder (ADHD)," *Gale Encyclopedia of Medicine.* Detroit: Gale, 2007. Reproduced by permission of Gale, a part of Cengage Learning.

and the inability to remain focused on tasks or activities.

ADHD, also known as hyperkinetic disorder (HKD) outside of the United States, is estimated to affect 3–9% of children, and affects boys about three times more often than girls. Although difficult to assess in infancy and toddlerhood, signs of ADHD may begin to appear as early as age two or three. The symptom picture tends to change as adolescence approaches. Many symptoms, particularly hyperactivity, diminish in early adulthood, but impulsivity and inattention problems remain with up to 50% of ADHD individuals throughout their adult life.

The first step in determining if a child has ADHD is to consult with a pediatrician for an accurate diagnosis. (© age fotostock/ SuperStock)

FAST FACT

According to the National Center for Health Statistics, about 4.7 million children between the ages of three and seventeen had ADHD in 2006.

Children with ADHD have short attention spans, becoming easily bored and/or frustrated with tasks. Although they may be quite intelligent, their lack of focus frequently results in poor grades and difficulties in school. They may often act impulsively, taking action first and thinking later, and are often constantly moving, running, climbing, squirming, and fidgeting. Many children with ADHD have trouble with gross and fine motor skills and, as a result, may be physically clumsy and awkward. Their clumsiness may extend to the social arena, where they are sometimes shunned due to their impulsive and intrusive behavior.

Causes and Symptoms

The causes of ADHD are not known. However, it appears that heredity plays a major role. Children with a parent or sibling with ADHD are more likely to develop the disorder themselves. Scientists have identified at least 20 candidate genes that might contribute to ADHD, but no single gene stands out as the gene causing the condition. Before birth, children with ADHD may have been exposed to poor maternal nutrition, viral infections, or maternal substance abuse. In early childhood, exposure to lead or other toxins can cause ADHD-like symptoms. Traumatic brain injury or neurological disorders may also trigger ADHD symptoms. Although the exact cause of ADHD is not known, an imbalance of certain neurotransmitters, the chemicals in the brain that transmit messages between nerve cells, is believed to be the mechanism behind its symptoms.

A widely publicized study conducted by Dr. Ben Feingold in the early 1970s suggested that allergies to certain foods and food additives caused the characteristic hyperactivity of children with ADHD. Although some children may have adverse reactions to certain foods that can affect their behavior (for example, a rash might temporarily cause a child to be distracted from other tasks), carefully controlled follow-up studies have uncovered no link between food allergies and ADHD. Another popularly held misconception about food and ADHD is that the consumption of sugar causes hyperactive behavior. Again, studies have shown no link between sugar intake and ADHD. It is important to note, however, that a nutritionally balanced diet is important for normal development in *all* children.

Psychologists and other mental health professionals typically use the criteria listed in the *Diagnostic and Statistical Manual of Mental Disorders, Fourth Edition (DSM-IV)* as a guideline for determining the presence of ADHD. For a diagnosis of ADHD, *DSM-IV* requires the presence of at least six of the following symptoms of inattention, or six or more symptoms of hyperactivity and impulsivity combined:

Inattention:

- fails to pay close attention to detail or makes careless mistakes in schoolwork or other activities
- has difficulty sustaining attention in tasks or activities
- does not appear to listen when spoken to
- does not follow through on instructions and does not finish tasks
- has difficulty organizing tasks and activities
- avoids or dislikes tasks that require sustained mental effort (e.g., homework)
- is easily distracted
- is forgetful in daily activities

Hyperactivity:

- fidgets with hands or feet or squirms in seat

- does not remain seated when expected to
- runs or climbs excessively when inappropriate (in adolescents and adults, feelings of restlessness)
- has difficulty playing quietly
- is constantly on the move
- talks excessively

Impulsivity:

- blurts out answers before the question has been completed
- has difficulty waiting for his or her turn
- interrupts and/or intrudes on others

Diagnosis

The first step in determining if a child has ADHD is to consult with a pediatrician. The pediatrician can make an initial evaluation of the child's developmental maturity compared to other children in his or her age group. The physician should also perform a comprehensive physical examination to rule out any organic causes of ADHD symptoms, such as an overactive thyroid or vision or hearing problems.

If no organic problem can be found, a psychologist, psychiatrist, neurologist, neuropsychologist, or learning specialist is typically consulted to perform a comprehensive ADHD assessment. A complete medical, family, social, psychiatric, and educational history is compiled from existing medical and school records and from interviews with parents and teachers. Interviews may also be conducted with the child, depending on his or her age. Along with these interviews, several clinical inventories may also be used, such as the Conners Rating Scales (Teacher's Questionnaire and Parent's Questionnaire), Child Behavior Checklist (CBCL), and the Achenbach Child Behavior Rating Scales. These inventories provide valuable information about the child's behavior in different settings and situations. In addition, the Wender Utah Rating Scale has been adapted for use in diagnosing ADHD in adults.

It is important to note that mental disorders such as depression and anxiety disorder can cause symptoms similar to ADHD. A complete and comprehensive psychiatric assessment is critical to differentiate ADHD from other possible mood and behavioral disorders. Bipolar disorder, for example, may be misdiagnosed as ADHD.

Public schools are required by federal law to offer free ADHD testing upon request. A pediatrician can also provide a referral to a psychologist or pediatric specialist for ADHD assessment. Parents should check with their insurance plans to see if these services are covered.

Treatment

Psychosocial therapy, usually combined with medications, is the treatment approach of choice to alleviate ADHD symptoms. Psychostimulants, such as dextroamphetamine (Dexedrine), pemoline (Cylert), and methylphenidate (Ritalin) are commonly prescribed to control hyperactive and impulsive behavior and increase attention span. They work by stimulating the production of certain neurotransmitters in the brain. Possible side effects of stimulants include nervous tics, irregular heartbeat, loss of appetite, and insomnia. However, the medications are usually well-tolerated and safe in most cases.

In 2004, the American Academy of Child and Adolescent Psychiatry listed the first nonstimulant as a first-line therapy for ADHD. Called atomoxetine HCl (Strattera), it is a norepinephrine reuptake inhibitor. This means that it helps to prevent the neurotransmitter norepinephrine [from being] reabsorbed into the cells of the brain.

In children who do not respond well to stimulant therapy, tricyclic antidepressants such as desipramine (Norpramin, Pertofane) and amitriptyline (Elavil) are sometimes recommended. Reported side effects of these

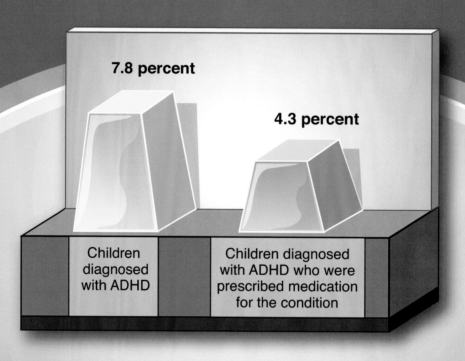

Children Diagnosed with ADHD and Prescribed Medication, 2003

7.8 percent

4.3 percent

Children diagnosed with ADHD

Children diagnosed with ADHD who were prescribed medication for the condition

Taken from: Susana N. Visser et al., "Medical Estimates and Factors Associated with Medication Treatment for Childhood Attention Deficit Hyperactivity Disorder," *Pediatrics*, February 2007.

drugs include persistent dry mouth, sedation, disorientation, and cardiac arrhythmia (particularly with desipramine). Other medications prescribed for ADHD therapy include buproprion (Wellbutrin), an antidepressant; fluoxetine (Prozac), an SSRI [selective serotonin reuptake inhibitor] antidepressant; and carbamazepine (Tegretol, Atretol), an anticonvulsant drug. Clonidine (Catapres), an antihypertensive medication, has also been used to control aggression and hyperactivity in some ADHD children, although it should not be used with Ritalin. A child's response to medication will change with age and maturation, so ADHD symptoms should be monitored closely and prescriptions adjusted accordingly.

Behavior modification therapy uses a reward system to reinforce good behavior and task completion and can be implemented both in the classroom and at home. A tangible reward such as a sticker may be given to the child every time he completes a task or behaves in an acceptable manner. A chart system may be used to display the stickers and visually illustrate the child's progress. When a certain number of stickers are collected, the child may trade them in for a bigger reward such as a trip to the zoo or a day at the beach. The reward system stays in place until the good behavior becomes ingrained.

A variation of this technique, cognitive-behavioral therapy, works to decrease impulsive behavior by getting the child to recognize the connection between thoughts and behavior, and to change behavior by changing negative thinking patterns.

Individual psychotherapy can help children with ADHD build self-esteem, give them a place to discuss their worries and anxieties, and help them gain insight into their behavior and feelings. Family therapy may also be beneficial in helping family members develop coping skills and in working through feelings of guilt or anger they may be experiencing.

Children with ADHD perform better within a familiar, consistent, and structured routine with positive reinforcements for good behavior and real consequences for bad behavior. Family, friends, and caretakers should all be educated about the special needs and behaviors of the child. Communication between parents and teachers is especially critical to ensuring that a child with ADHD has an appropriate learning environment.

Alternative Treatment

A number of alternative treatments exist for ADHD. Although there is a lack of controlled studies to prove their efficacy, proponents report that they are successful in controlling symptoms in some ADHD patients. Some of the more popular alternative treatments include:

- EEG (electroencephalograph) biofeedback. By measuring brainwave activity and teaching the patient which type of brainwave is associated with attention, EEG biofeedback attempts to train patients to generate the desired brainwave activity.

- Dietary therapy. Based in part on the Feingold food allergy diet, dietary therapy focuses on a nutritional plan that is high in protein and complex carbohydrates and free of white sugar and salicylate-containing foods such as strawberries, tomatoes, and grapes.

- Herbal therapy. Herbal therapy uses a variety of natural remedies to address the symptoms of ADHD, such as ginkgo (*Ginkgo biloba*) for memory and mental sharpness and chamomile (*Matricaria recutita*) extract for calming. The safety of herbal remedies has not been demonstrated in controlled studies. For example, it is known that ginkgo may affect blood coagulation, but controlled studies have not yet evaluated the risk of the effect.

- Homeopathic medicine. The theory of homeopathic medicine is to treat the whole person at a core level. Constitutional homeopathic care requires consulting with a well-trained homeopath who has experience working with individuals who have ADHD.

Prognosis

Untreated, ADHD negatively affects a child's social and educational performance and can seriously damage his or her sense of self-esteem. Children with ADHD often have impaired relationships with their peers, and may be looked upon as social outcasts. They may be perceived as slow learners or troublemakers in the classroom. Siblings and even parents may develop resentful feelings towards the child with ADHD.

Some children with ADHD also develop a conduct disorder problem. For those adolescents who have both ADHD and a conduct disorder, as many as 25% go on to develop antisocial personality disorder and the criminal behavior, substance abuse, and high rate of suicide attempts that are symptomatic of it. Children diagnosed with ADHD are also more likely to have a learning disorder, a mood disorder such as depression, and an anxiety disorder.

Approximately 70–80% of patients with ADHD who are treated with stimulant medication experience significant relief from symptoms, at least in the short-term. Approximately one-half of children with ADHD seem to "outgrow" the disorder in adolescence or early adulthood; the other half will retain some or all symptoms of ADHD as adults. With early identification and intervention, careful compliance with a treatment program, and a supportive and nurturing home and school environment, children with ADHD can flourish socially and academically.

Many Adults Have ADHD

Diana Mahoney

In the following viewpoint Diana Mahoney discusses the prevalence of adult attention deficit hyperactivity disorder (ADHD). According to Mahoney, studies have shown that ADHD—once considered a child-hood disease—is common in adults as well. Many children with ADHD never grow out of the disorder. Additionally, some people with ADHD are not even diagnosed until they are adults. Some of the many difficulties faced by adults with ADHD include substance abuse, depression, and anxiety. Mahoney thinks more should be done to identify adults with ADHD and get them the treatment they need. Diana Mahoney is a medical writer.

In their best-selling book *Driven to Distraction*, Dr. Edward M. Hallowell and Dr. John J. Ratey gave voice to what thousands of inattentive, impulsive, restless adults had thought to themselves for years: "I have a

SOURCE: Diana Mahoney, "Adults with ADHD Need to Know Treatment Options," *Clinical Psychiatry News,* vol. 35, September 2007, p. 30. Copyright © 2007 International Medical News Group. Reproduced by permission.

problem." And their problem had a familiar name—attention-deficit/hyperactivity disorder.

The authors were not the first to consider the possibility of ADD in adults, but *Driven to Distraction* was among the first to popularize for a lay audience the idea that attention-deficit disorder (ADD) with or without hyperactivity is frequently a lifelong condition associated with a broad spectrum of negative consequences.

ADHD Adults Are More Likely to Self-Medicate

Multiple studies have shown that adults with ADD or ADHD typically have moderate to extreme difficulties in functioning at work, home, or school. Additionally, people who struggle with the disorder are more likely to "self-medicate" with alcohol or drugs and to have higher rates of substance abuse problems. They also are significantly more likely to suffer from depression and anxiety, to be fired from jobs, and to get divorced, compared with adults without the disorders.

In a longitudinal study in Sweden that followed a sample of children with ADHD into adulthood, a blinded assessment of psychiatric status showed that 49% of the adults who had been diagnosed with the disorder as children continued to have marked symptoms of the condition at age 22, and 58% met the criteria for having a poor outcome—which included drug or alcohol misuse, living off a disability pension or welfare benefits, major personality disorder, chronic severe psychiatric disorder, or conviction for a criminal offense.

Even seemingly successful adults with ADHD, which occurs at every level of intelligence, do worse occupationally than their peers without the condition. In one controlled study of functional impairments associated with adult ADHD, those adults with a self-reported ADHD diagnosis were significantly less likely to have graduated high school, obtained a college degree, or be currently employed than age- and gender-matched adults in the community without ADHD. Also, they were significantly less satisfied with their family, social, and professional lives.

Number of Adults with ADHD Is Substantial and May Be Under-Estimated

Given current prevalence estimates, the number of adults at risk for such outcomes is substantial. The results of a screen for adult ADHD in the United States based on a probability subsample of 3,199 respondents between the ages of 18 and 44 in the *National Comorbidity Survey Replication* showed an estimated adult ADHD prevalence of 4.4%.

Similarly, the recent World Health Organization World Mental Survey Initiative, which screened more than 11,000 adults between the ages of 18 and 44 from North and South America, Europe, and the Middle East, showed an estimated prevalence of adult ADHD of 3.4%, ranging from 1.2% to 7.3%.

In both studies, ADHD was highly comorbid with other *DSM-IV* [*Diagnostic and Statistical Manual of Mental Disorders*] disorders and was associated with considerable role disability.

Some experts suggest the published prevalence numbers underestimate the true burden of adult ADHD, and argue that the *DSM-IV* diagnostic criterion that symptoms be present before age 7 is too stringent and does not take into account individuals with later onset of the condition. "The age-of-onset criterion for ADHD in *DSM-IV* is based on clinical wisdom and on the belief that ADHD is a childhood-onset disorder," said Stephen V. Faraone, PhD, of the State University of New York [Upstate Medical Center in] Syracuse.

In fact, Dr. Faraone and his colleagues recently demonstrated that individuals with a later onset of symptoms experience similar short- and longer-term outcomes as those with onset before age 7. The investigators compared 127 adults with full ADHD who met all of the *DSM-IV* criteria for childhood-onset ADHD with 79 subjects with late-onset ADHD who met all of the criteria except age of onset (approximately 80% of the individuals in the latter group were aged 7–12 at diagnosis). They determined that both groups had similar patterns of psychiatric comorbidity, functional impairment, and familial transmission.

Adults with ADHD are more likely to self-medicate with drugs and/or alcohol.
(© Francisco Cruz/ SuperStock)

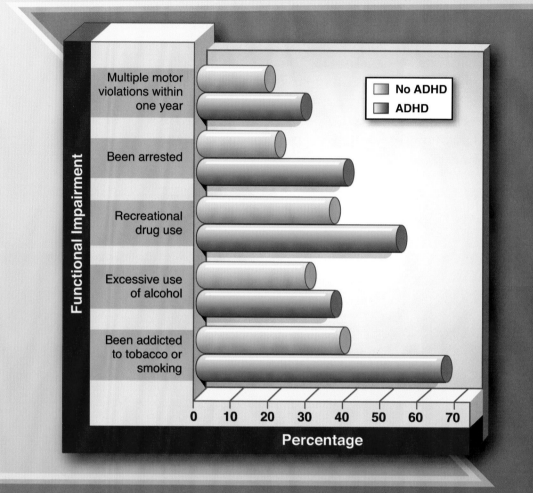

Adults with ADHD Have Significant Functional Impairment

Functional Impairment

Multiple motor violations within one year

Been arrested

Recreational drug use

Excessive use of alcohol

Been addicted to tobacco or smoking

No ADHD
ADHD

0   10   20   30   40   50   60   70

Percentage

Taken from: American Society of Addiction Medicine, "ADHD and Co-occurring Substance Use Disorders: New Clinical Insights and Emerging Therapies," October 1, 2007.

Many Adults Do Not Receive Treatment

Regardless of age of onset, most adults with ADHD do not receive treatment for the condition, despite evidence supporting the efficacy of pharmacologic and behavioral interventions. In the aforementioned prevalence studies, about 10% of those respondents with adult ADHD reported receiving treatment for it, and when treatment did occur, the most common reason for seeking it was a comorbid disorder, not ADHD.

These findings suggest that adult ADHD is not well recognized and is undertreated in the community, according to Dr. Anthony Rostain, director of the Adult Developmental Disorders Unit of the University of Pennsylvania, Philadelphia. They also underscore the need for more careful screening, particularly in adult patients receiving treatment for depression, anxiety, and substance abuse, he said.

When adults with ADHD do seek help, those with psychiatric comorbidity are significantly more likely to receive either behavioral therapy or combined behavioral and ADHD-specific pharmacotherapy than those individuals without psychiatric comorbidity, according to a 2006 study at the University of Nebraska, Omaha, that examined medication and behavioral treatment of adult ADHD in U.S. ambulatory care between 1996–2003.

In the absence of psychiatric comorbidity, adults being treated for ADHD are significantly more likely to receive pharmacotherapy alone, wrote Jayashri Sankaranarayanan, PhD, and her colleagues.

Several recent studies have suggested that these patients might be better served through combination treatment with medication and behavioral therapy.

Medication Plus Behavioral Therapy Is Effective

At the University of Pennsylvania, for example, Dr. Rostain and colleagues examined the clinical outcomes of 43 adult patients in the Adult ADHD Treatment and Research Program who were prescribed combination therapy consisting of treatment with mixed salts of amphetamine and participation in 16 individual cognitive-behavioral therapy (CBT) sessions that were each 50 minutes long. The CBT comprised psychoeducation about ADHD, patient-centered conceptualizations of patients'

FAST FACT

About 4.4 percent of American adults have ADHD, according to a 2006 study reported in the *American Journal of Psychiatry*.

associated difficulties, coping strategies, behavior modification techniques, and the identification of supportive resources. Significant improvements were observed in all clinical measures of ADHD symptom severity and overall functioning, independent of any demographic or clinical variables, according to the authors.

In a Massachusetts General Hospital study, Dr. Steven A. Safren and his colleagues demonstrated that medication plus ADHD-focused CBT, initiated after medication stabilization, produces greater symptom reduction than medication alone. "Most individuals treated with medication continue to have evidence [of] at least some residual symptoms and functional impairments, which are often amenable to a structured, cognitive-behavioral treatment approach," Dr. Safren said.

The data on adult ADHD are still limited, compared with childhood ADHD, but researchers and clinicians have begun addressing, in earnest, an important question: What happens when the wiggly, distracted, rambunctious kids with ADHD grow up? Ideally, the answer should be that they are offered the help they need.

Girls Also Suffer from ADHD

Nicole Crawford

In the following viewpoint Nicole Crawford talks with several leading psychologists who are trying to raise awareness about females with attention deficit hyperactivity disorder (ADHD). The psychologists say that ADHD is often overlooked in girls because their ADHD symptoms differ from boys' symptoms. Whereas girls tend to have the "inattentive" type of ADHD, boys tend to have the "hyperactive" type. According to Crawford, girls with ADHD face many difficulties in life and typically are not diagnosed until after they have children themselves. Nicole Crawford is a writer for *Monitor on Psychology*, a publication of the American Psychological Association.

When psychologist Stephen P. Hinshaw, PhD, published two studies on attention-deficit hyperactivity disorder (ADHD) in girls last October [2002], psychologist Kathleen Nadeau, PhD, was

SOURCE: Nicole Crawford, "ADHD: A Women's Issue," *Monitor on Psychology*, vol. 34, February 2003, p. 28. Copyright © 2003 American Psychological Association. Reproduced by permission.

A young girl with ADHD is inattentive in class. ADHD is often overlooked in girls because their symptoms differ from those of boys. (© Butch Martin/Alamy)

heartened that females with ADHD were finally beginning to receive long overdue attention from researchers.

"Hinshaw is one of the first to study girls themselves," says Nadeau of the lead author's work, published in the *Journal of Consulting and Clinical Psychology*. "Most of the few prior studies have focused on comparing girls to boys—using boys' ADHD symptoms as the marker against which girls should be measured."

Girls Are Overlooked and Undiagnosed

For Nadeau, Hinshaw's research was vindication for what she had observed clinically for years: "that girls experience significant struggles that are often overlooked because their ADHD symptoms bear little resemblance to those of boys." It was also a signal for her to push even harder to raise the awareness of the needs of women with the disorder. Through advocacy and groundbreaking research and writing, Nadeau and a small group of psychologists are fighting to bring the issues of ADHD in women from the fringes of research to center stage.

"Historically, research on ADHD has focused almost exclusively on hyperactive little boys, and only in the past six or seven years has any research focused on adult ADHD," says Nadeau, an expert on the disorder in women and director of Chesapeake Psychological Services of Maryland in Silver Spring. "And the recognition of females [with the disorder] has lagged even further behind."

According to Nadeau, this lagging recognition of girls and women is due to current diagnostic criteria—which remain more appropriate for males than females—and to parent and teacher referral patterns, spurred by the more obvious and more problematic male ADHD behaviors. Some deny that the disorder exists in females—or in anyone at all.

Researcher and educational therapist Jane Adelizzi, PhD, theorizes that females with ADHD have been largely neglected by researchers because hyperactivity is usually missing in girls, who typically have attention deficit disorder (ADD), the inattentive type of ADHD. But for advocates, the bottom line is this: Girls with undiagnosed ADHD will most likely carry their problems into adulthood, and left untreated, their lives often fall apart.

"Girls with untreated ADHD are at risk for chronic low self-esteem, underachievement, anxiety, depression, teen pregnancy, early smoking during middle school and high school," says Nadeau.

As adults, they're at risk for "divorce, financial crises, single-parenting a child with ADHD, never completing college, underemployment, substance abuse, eating disorders and constant stress due to difficulty in managing the demands of daily life—which overflow into the difficulties of their children, 50 percent of whom are likely to have ADHD as well," Nadeau adds.

"Girls with ADHD remain an enigma—often overlooked, misunderstood and hotly debated," says Ellen Littman, PhD, one of the first psychologists and researchers to focus on gender differences in ADHD and to advocate for a re-examination of how the disorder is defined.

Littman theorizes that girls with ADHD aren't identified and helped earlier in their lives because male ADHD patterns have been over-represented in the literature. "As with all diversity issues, the danger lies in assuming that these more typical patterns characterize all children with ADHD," says Littman, who runs a clinical practice in Mount Kisco, N.Y. "Therefore, while there appears to be an abundance of information available on ADHD, we may have a false sense that we know more about the experience of girls with ADHD than we really do."

More research on gender issues in ADHD is needed for several reasons, says Julia J. Rucklidge, PhD, assistant psychology professor at the University of Canterbury in Christchurch, New Zealand, who has studied ADHD in Canadian women. "We can't make assumptions that what applies to males will apply to females—females have different hormonal influences to start with that can greatly affect their behavior." Also, Rucklidge says, females are socialized differently and therefore tend to express themselves in a different manner, and are more susceptible to such problems as depression or anxiety that again influence behavior. This suggests that ADHD "will manifest and express itself differently in females," she says. "But only research can tell us this definitively. Until then, these are assumptions that we make."

Many Women Are Not Diagnosed Until After They Become Mothers

Many women are in their late 30s or early 40s before they are diagnosed with ADHD. "One of the most common pathways to a woman being diagnosed is that one of her children is diagnosed. She begins to educate herself and recognizes traits in herself," says Nadeau. "These women are [usually] going to be older," because children are typically diagnosed with ADHD in mid-to-late elementary school.

Women with ADHD typically present with tremendous time management challenges, chronic disorganization, longstanding feelings of stress and being overwhelmed, difficulties with money management, children or siblings with ADHD, and a history of anxiety and depression, says Nadeau, who didn't recognize her own

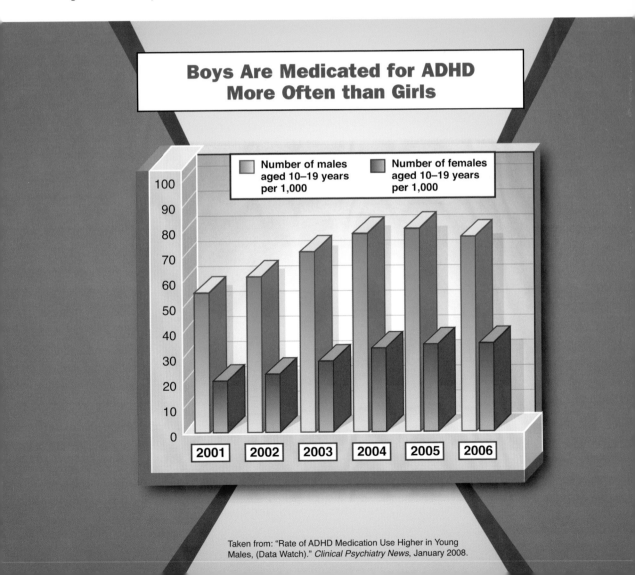

Boys Are Medicated for ADHD More Often than Girls

Number of males aged 10–19 years per 1,000

Number of females aged 10–19 years per 1,000

Taken from: "Rate of ADHD Medication Use Higher in Young Males, (Data Watch)." *Clinical Psychiatry News*, January 2008.

ADHD until middle age and has a daughter and a brother with the condition.

The disorder is typically treated with a combination of stimulant medication and ADHD-focused psychotherapy, "which is very structured, goal-oriented, and uses many 'coaching' techniques, as well as standard psychotherapy techniques," says Nadeau. "Women more than men with ADHD struggle with low self-esteem, and this needs to be a major focus of therapy," she adds.

FAST FACT

From 2004 to 2006, about 4.8 percent of American girls aged six to seventeen had ADHD, compared with 11.8 percent of American boys aged six to seventeen, according to the U.S. Centers for Disease Control and Prevention.

Many of the women who come to clinical and neuropsychologist Mitchell Clionsky, PhD, for ADHD testing fit the typical profile. One 42-year-old patient he diagnosed with ADD was referred by a psychiatrist treating her for depression. Her marriage was troubled, and she had low self-esteem, says Clionsky, the cofounder of the ADD Center of Western Massachusetts in Springfield. Since childhood, the patient had thought she was lazy and irresponsible because she didn't complete things she started. A "very bright woman," she completed a few years of college, and "probably would have gone farther had her problem been identified sooner," he says.

The tragedy is "these are people significantly underachieving and [who] end up going the depression route, mostly the result of life failure," Clionsky says. "It's like they're running life's race with lead weights on their ankles."

Pioneering Research Reveals Difficulties Women with ADHD Face

Some psychologists are building up the literature on ADHD among women. Julia Rucklidge began studying the area while working on her doctorate in psychology at the University of Calgary in Alberta, Canada. "When I started in 1995, there was very little research in the adult population [and] maybe one or two studies looking specifically at women with ADD," she says.

Rucklidge, with colleague Bonnie Kaplan, PhD, studied 102 women ages 26 to 59, with a mean age of 41. Half of the women interviewed had ADHD and half did not. All of the women in the study had a child with ADHD—therefore all subjects could relate to the stressors involved in parenting a child with the disorder.

Rucklidge's findings, published in the *Journal of Attention Disorders* and the *Journal of Clinical Psychology*, shed light on the experiences of women diagnosed in adulthood:

- Women with ADHD were more likely to have a "learned helpless style" of responding to negative situations than were women without the disorder and tended to blame themselves when bad things happened.

- Women with ADHD were likely to believe that they couldn't control the outcomes of life events, resulting in a vicious cycle, reports Rucklidge. "A woman with ADHD is less likely to make efforts to finish challenging tasks due to her belief that she has no power to change the negative outcome. By giving up, she further reinforces the belief that she is unable to accomplish things in life," she says.

- Women with ADHD were also more likely to report a history of depression and anxiety. They had also been in psychological treatment more often and had received more prescriptions for psychotropic medications than had women without ADHD.

Jane Adelizzi's research explored a rarely mined area of ADHD: its similarity to post-traumatic stress disorder (PTSD). Three of her studies looked at women diagnosed with attention and learning problems who also showed PTSD symptoms as a result of experiencing classroom trauma—which she defines as a significantly unpleasant external event or stressor occurring within the confines of an educational environment that is of a psychological nature.

"As a result of classroom trauma over a span of years, some women develop a set of symptoms that are recognizable—by some professionals—as post-traumatic stress symptoms," reports Adelizzi, coordinator of the Adult Center, Program for the Advancement of Learning at Curry College in Milton, Mass. "These symptoms are also similar—too similar—to ADHD behaviors and symptoms."

It's not always clear which comes first, the post-traumatic stress symptoms, the ADHD symptoms or the trauma, says Adelizzi. But, she argues, these women's ADHD symptoms can't be helped without looking into the coexisting panic and anxiety that can be triggered many years later—if, for example, they decide to return to school.

Raising Awareness

In addition to pushing for more studies on gender issues, these psychologists use a range of forums to raise awareness of ADHD in women. With pediatrician Patricia Quinn, MD, Nadeau . . . founded the National Center for Gender Issues and ADHD (NCGI) to promote awareness and research on the disorder in females.

ADHD Is Related to Delayed Brain Growth

Lindsay Minnema

In the following selection Lindsay Minnema interviews scientists about the results of a study showing that attention deficit hyperactivity disorder (ADHD) may be associated with delayed brain growth. The study—which found that the brains of children with ADHD matured about three years later than the brains of children without the disorder—provides biological evidence for ADHD. It suggests that when ADHD brains "catch up" with normal brains, kids may no longer feel the symptoms of the disorder. The scientists who performed the study, however, say that they only looked at one part of the brain, and ADHD brains may still be different from normal brains in other areas. Lindsay Minnema is a writer for *The Washington Post* who specializes in health issues.

New findings that attention-deficit hyperactivity disorder may stem from a developmental delay that children could outgrow, rather than a cognitive deficit, have raised questions for parents of the 4.4 million children diagnosed with the disorder.

SOURCE: Lindsay Minnema, "Will Kids Outgrow ADHD?" www
.washingtonpost.com, November 27, 2007. Reprinted with permission.

The findings from a National Institute of Mental Health study, published online by the Proceedings of the National Academy of Sciences, compared brain scans of 446 children with and without the disorder. The brains of children with ADHD appeared to develop normally but more slowly, lagging on average about three years behind other children.

ADHD Was Long Suspected to Be Due to Developmental Delay

We spoke with several experts about what the findings might mean for parents.

Why the sudden change in thinking? It's not really sudden. Scientists have long suspected that ADHD may be tied to delays in brain development, but until now there has been little biological evidence. In the new study, biological differences were most evident in the cortex, the part of the brain that governs attention, planning and judgment. On average, in children with ADHD, thickening of the cortex appeared to peak at age 10.5, compared with age 7.5 in children without the disorder.

"It helps present a better, non-stigmatized, biological explanation for why . . . some kids have ADHD symptoms," said William Coleman, professor of developmental and behavioral pediatrics at the University of North Carolina and chairman of the Committee of Psychosocial Aspects of Child and Family Health at the American Academy of Pediatrics. "They're not bad, not lazy, not unmotivated. They don't have bad parents. They just have a developmental lag."

Some Brain Differences Do Not Go Away

Does this mean that my child will outgrow his ADHD symptoms by the time he's a teen? Perhaps.

"[The study] doesn't show that the brains of kids with ADHD completely 'normalize' by age 12 or so," the study's lead author, Philip Shaw, wrote in an e-mail [in November 2007]. "We only looked at one aspect of brain development. Many other structural and functional brain differences persist in the brains of teens with ADHD."

"While a lot of people with ADHD do improve with age, as many as two-thirds still have symptoms of the disorder which persist into adulthood," Shaw said. Among possible explanations: There may be more than one genetic variant of the disorder, or perhaps some kids with ADHD have other conditions that are responsible for their symptoms.

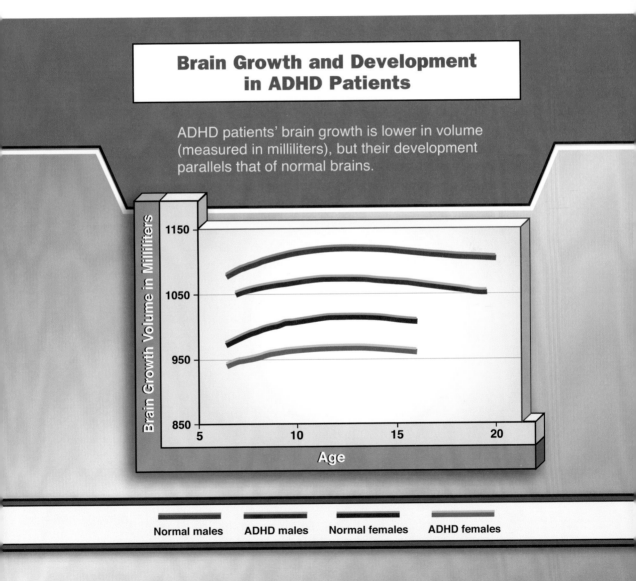

Brain Growth and Development in ADHD Patients

ADHD patients' brain growth is lower in volume (measured in milliliters), but their development parallels that of normal brains.

Normal males   ADHD males   Normal females   ADHD females

Taken from: NIMH Child Psychiatry Branch, October 8, 2002. www.nih.gov/news/pr/oct2002/nimh-08.htm.

While a lot of children with ADHD do improve with age, in nearly two-thirds of them the disorder's symptoms persist into adulthood. (Will and Deni McIntyre/ Photo Researchers, Inc.)

"The primary problem may be a learning disability," Coleman said. "[Researchers] say that once the cortex thickens, kids get better, but if they have ongoing, undiagnosed problems, their symptoms may persist."

Study Does Not Address Treatment

So, should I stop giving my child stimulant medications, such as Ritalin, to help with attention problems? That's beyond the reach of this latest study. "The study gives no implication of what treatments should be used," said Judith Rapoport, chief of the child psychiatry branch at the

National Institute of Mental Health and one of the authors of the study.

An estimated 2.5 million children in the United States took medications for ADHD in 2003, according to the Centers for Disease Control and Prevention.

Thomas Kobylski, past president of the Child and Adolescent Psychiatry Society of Greater Washington, says intervention with behavioral therapy or medication is important so that children don't fall behind academically or develop secondary problems, such as anxiety or low self-esteem.

> **FAST FACT**
>
> According to the National Resource Center on ADHD, about 60 percent of childhood cases of ADHD persist into adulthood.

"The field has clearly stated that delays are worrisome," he said. "You don't want kids to become more delayed. You don't want them to fall behind."

Whether medication is appropriate depends on a careful evaluation of a child's symptoms, environment, relationships and demands placed on him, Coleman said. "Always ask your physician: 'What is normal for my child developmentally?'"

Would it help to hold a child back in school so he can catch up to his peers? That depends, said Coleman, who generally advises against holding a child back in school for academic reasons alone. But if a child is feeling left out and is socially or emotionally behind his peers, it may benefit him to stay back a grade, he said.

There Is No Way to Speed Brain Growth, but Treatments Can Help

Isn't there a way to help nudge the development process along? Sadly, no. Adolescent brains are structurally different from children's brains, and there is no known way to speed up the growth process, Coleman said. What does help many children is a combination of medication and therapy—working closely with parents, teachers and physicians to help a child work through academic and social weaknesses.

ADHD Genes May Have Been Helpful for Ancient Nomads

William Saletan

In the following viewpoint William Saletan ponders the results of a study that indicates that the symptoms of attention deficit hyperactivity disorder (ADHD) may actually be helpful for certain populations. The study found that DRD4 7R, a gene that is linked to ADHD, seems to be helpful for nomadic tribesmen in Kenya, but it is disadvantageous for a different part of the tribe that has settled down and built a community. Saletan wonders whether this information may be useful in helping current society deal more effectively with children with ADHD. William Saletan is a writer for *Slate* magazine.

I s ADHD a disease?

The U.S. government says it is. So does the professional *Diagnostic & Statistical Manual for Mental Disorders (DMS)*. The condition's very name incorporates this assumption: attention-deficit/hyperactivity disorder. Lots of kids with ADHD have trouble functioning in modern society.

SOURCE: William Saletan, "New World Disorder," *Slate*, June 12, 2008. Distributed by United Feature Syndicate, Inc.

But what if society were different? What if it were structured so that having ADHD was actually an advantage?

This isn't some futuristic thought experiment. A new study suggests that this ADHD-friendly world may actually be part of our past.

ADHD Gene Provides Benefits for Certain Tribesmen

The study, led by Dan Eisenberg of Northwestern University and published in *BMC Evolutionary Biology*, examined a Kenyan tribe called the Ariaal. Part of the tribe has recently settled into an agricultural community. Another part remains nomadic. The tribesmen were tested for DRD4 7R, a genetic variant that, Eisenberg notes, "has been linked to greater food and drug cravings, novelty-seeking, and ADHD symptoms." He and his colleagues report:

> DRD4 7R+ genotypes were associated with indices of better nutritional status among nomads, particularly higher

A recent study of Kenyan tribesmen who were found to have the ADHD-linked gene variant DRD4 7R revealed that ADHD may actually be beneficial to nomadic tribes—although this did not prove true for settled tribes. (© **Yvette Cardozo/Alamy**)

fat free mass, but worse indices in the settled individuals. This suggests that the 7R allele confers additional adaptive benefits in the nomadic compared to sedentary context.

This difference, the authors report, is "consistent with past findings of higher 7R allele frequencies in nomadic populations around the world."

But how would the gene help nomads? The authors speculate:

> Increased impulsivity, ADHD-like traits, novelty-seeking like traits, aggression, violence and/or activity levels may help nomads obtain food resources, or exhibit a degree of behavioral unpredictability that is protective against interpersonal violence or robberies. . . . It might be that the attention spans conferred by the DRD4/7R+ genotype allow nomadic children to more readily learn effectively in a dynamic environment (without schools), while the same attention span interferes with classroom learning in Songa, the settled community. 7R+ boys might develop into warriors (the life-stage of an Ariaal male that lies between childhood and manhood) and men who can more effectively defend against livestock raiders, perhaps through a reputation of unpredictable behavior that inspires fear. Among 7R+ men in the settled community of Songa, such tendencies might be less well suited to practicing agriculture and selling goods at market. It might also be that higher activity levels in 7R+ nomads are translated into increased food production, while such activity levels in settled men are a less efficient use of calories in food production.

Remember, this is not a study of genetic differences between populations. The two Ariaal groups are genetically identical—the agricultural group became settled only 35

FAST FACT

ADHD has a "heritability rate" of 76 percent, meaning that 76 percent of the variability of ADHD in the entire population is due to genetics, according to genetics professor Susan Smalley of the University of California–Los Angeles.

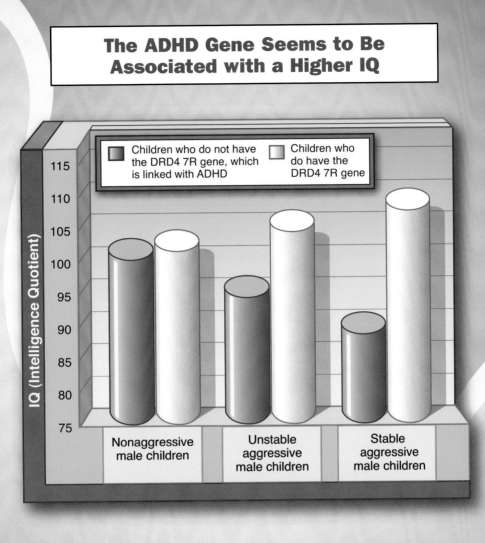

The ADHD Gene Seems to Be Associated with a Higher IQ

Children who do not have the DRD4 7R gene, which is linked with ADHD

Children who do have the DRD4 7R gene

IQ (Intelligence Quotient)

115
110
105
100
95
90
85
80
75

Nonaggressive male children

Unstable aggressive male children

Stable aggressive male children

Taken from: Colin G. DeYoung et al., "The Dopamine D4 Receptor Gene and the Modernization of the Association Between Externalizing Behavior and IQ," *Archives of General Psychiatry*, December 2006.

years ago—and the groups intermarry. The difference lies in their lifestyles. The point of the study is that the same gene has different effects in different settings.

Society Can Adapt to Genes Instead of the Other Way Around

I don't know whether the speculated reasons for the gene's benefits will pan out. But the benefits do seem real. And that finding suggests two things. First, we should be careful about designating diseases and disease genes. Traits that are harmful in one setting can be helpful in another. Advantages or "defects" that we think of as natural may actually be products of our cultural decisions. As Eisenberg puts it, we might "begin to view ADHD as not just a disease but something with adaptive components."

Second, our society may be the wrong place to assess a gene's evolutionary harm or benefit. As the authors note, "[N]on-industrialized or subsistence environments . . . may be more similar to the environments where much of human genetic evolution took place."

This doesn't mean ADHD is wonderful. Genes that promote fat storage may have been similarly advantageous in subsistence environments, but obesity is still a curse. The lesson of the Ariaal study is simply that society can adapt to genes instead of the other way around. Maybe we don't have to screen and chuck embryos for every "disease" gene, or drug the kids once they're born. Maybe we can put ADHD kids in educational settings more like the dynamic environment of our nomad forebears. And maybe we can raise kids with fat-storage genes in settings less full of food.

If it wasn't too hard for our ancestors, is it really too hard for us?

Brain Imaging May Help Diagnose and Treat ADHD

Claire Shipman and Ariane Nalty

In the following viewpoint Claire Shipman and Ariane Nalty describe how brain imaging techniques such as electroencephalography (EEG) and magnetic resonance imaging (MRI) may be able to help doctors diagnose attention deficit hyperactivity disorder (ADHD). Brain imaging can also reveal nuances in brain function that can help doctors design the most effective treatments. Some doctors are skeptical that brain imaging is worth the cost. However, Shipman and Nalty describe how treatments based on brain imaging have made a world of difference in the lives of some children with ADHD. Claire Shipman and Ariane Nalty are national correspondents for ABC News.

Two million American children have been diagnosed with attention deficit hyperactivity disorder [ADHD], according to the National Institute of Mental Health. It's so common now that one child in a

SOURCE: Claire Shipman and Ariane Nalty, "Looking Inside Kids' Minds Can Open the Future," ABC News, May 20, 2008. Reproduced by permission.

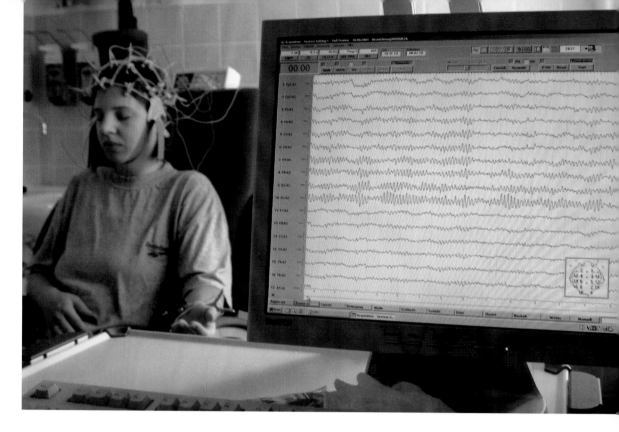

A patient undergoes electroencephalography (EEG) at a neurologist's office. The authors say that EEGs and MRIs (magnetic resonance imaging) help doctors diagnose ADHD. (Klaus Rose/dpa/Landov)

classroom of 25 or 30 will have the disorder. But parents often struggle a long time to figure out exactly what's going on in their child's head. Is he tired? Is she confused? Is he just acting up? Does she need help?

Dr. Fernando Miranda, a neurologist at the Bright Minds Institute in San Francisco, says diagnosing children with behavioral disorders like ADHD and autism without looking at their brains is like trying to diagnose heart problems without actually looking at the heart.

On the other hand, some of Miranda's patients have found they had an attention deficit problem and didn't even know it. Miranda, and many other doctors, believe more objective tools for figuring out these puzzles are critical.

Brain Scans Show a Child Has an Attention Problem

From an early age, 9-year-old Danny Rodgers had trouble speaking.

Danny's words were in his head; they just couldn't seem to find a way out. Embarrassed, he avoided talking altogether and stopped trying to make friends.

Danny's grandparents, Jeanne and Howard Rodgers, who have been raising him and his sister, Meghan, since their mother died, said the school system recommended speech therapy, and patience.

"They kept saying, 'He'll grow out of it. He'll grow out of it,'" said Jeanne Rodgers.

But he never did.

"He'd cry a lot and say, 'I don't like my life. I don't like what I'm doing. I don't want to go to school,'" said Danny's grandmother.

They went to see Miranda at the Bright Minds Institute, and Miranda took a different approach to treating Danny.

Danny was wired for a quantitative electroencephalography, or EEG, a very sophisticated test that measures a brain's electrical output in response to certain stimuli. He also underwent a comprehensive neuropsychological exam, and magnetic resonance imaging of the brain.

Those tests revealed a lot of surprises.

"This child's IQ was 138," Miranda said. "And that's huge. That's so bright."

One EEG measurement, called a P300, showed normal and abnormal electrical impulses in Danny's brain with a series of bright colors. Reading the scan, Miranda said Danny was not "perceiving" speech in the superior temporal gyrus.

> ## FAST FACT
>
> In June 2008 the National Institute of Mental Health announced that it was funding a study into the effectiveness of using electroencephalography biofeedback training to treat ADHD.

Translation: Danny has what's known as an auditory processing issue. It wasn't so much that he was having trouble speaking or pronouncing things—his brain wasn't understanding speech correctly. Danny's problem was not a standard speech issue at all, and his years of conventional therapy were off target.

Miranda pointed out a group of squiggly lines on the scan, showing Danny was likely to have an attention problem. In a normal EEG, those squiggly lines would not be there in the frontal lobe section of this recording. Using those tests and other physical and behavioral information, Miranda diagnosed Danny with ADHD.

"The areas of the brain that are involved in attention deficits are many, and unless you know which one specifically is the one that you're addressing, that is not functioning very well, you cannot prescribe the right medication for it," Miranda said.

For Danny, that meant the puzzle was solved in ways his grandparents never would have guessed. "He wasn't a hyper child at all," Jeanne Rodgers said.

Now on ADHD medication and specific therapy for his decoding problem, Danny has a lot to say. "I didn't like learning. I thought it was boring," Danny admitted in Miranda's office. But now "it's kind of fun," he said.

"He got nine out of 10 'outstandings' on his report card!" his grandmother marveled.

Danny's unhappiness used to tear up his grandparents. Jeanne Rodgers and her husband, Howard, are spending all they can on his special therapy, and have also spent a bundle on the tests with Miranda, almost none of which were covered by insurance. But both of them said the costs have been well worth it.

Some Doctors Dispute That Brain Tests Can Diagnose ADHD

Still, some leading doctors say it's too soon to use sophisticated tests like these clinically, and that people might be wasting their money on them.

Dr. Bradley Peterson, director of the Pediatric Neuropsychiatry Research program at Columbia College of Physicians and Surgeons, said the technology is not there yet.

"No test can tell you that this child has ADHD and that one doesn't," Peterson said. "At least at present day. Hopefully, in the next year or coming years, we might have that, but we don't yet."

Others who work with the technology routinely, such as Dr. Sandlan Lowe, a professor in the departments of psychiatry, physiology and neuroscience at New York University School of Medicine, said it can help in reaching a diagnosis.

"In Europe, for instance, EEG and quantitative EEG is routinely done," Lowe said. "In this country, I think there are a lot of neurologists who have the idea that it's just not that helpful. And I have to tell you that in the right hands, it's a very useful tool."

So why isn't it used more often? A number of doctors said reading the MRIs and EEGs is complicated, and not every neurologist is properly trained to read them. The tests are also expensive, and are often not covered by insurance.

Many scam artists have also claimed they could read these brain imaging tests when they could not, bilking people out of thousands of dollars.

But Miranda, as well as many patients, believe they are on the cutting edge of a new frontier in diagnosing and treating children's cognitive problems.

Brain Tests Can Reveal Details That Help Doctors Prescribe the Best Treatment

Jan Jensen, a nurse whose husband is a surgeon, worried about the attention problems she saw in her three children. But she wasn't happy that her family practictioner suggested prescribing Ritalin without doing any tests.

Lindsey, 12, always seemed restless and unfocused, Jensen said. Megan, 8, was having significant trouble reading. But Jensen was especially worried about 9-year-old Zach.

Basics About Brain Imaging Techniques

	When it became clinically available	What it uses	What it shows	Radioactivity used?	Typical price	Number of accredited facilities in United States
Computed Tomography (CT)	1970s	X-rays	Brain structure	Yes	$300 to $950	2,746
Magnetic Resonance Imaging (MRI)	1980s	Radio waves	Brain structure	No	$800 to $2,000	4,937
Positron Emission Tomography (PET)	1990s	Gamma rays	Brain function	Yes	$3,000 to $6,000	702

[Compiled by editor.]

"He's like the energizer bunny on crack. I'm telling you, this kid is constantly going," she said, adding he has almost no fear and little ability to understand the consequences of his actions.

All three had MRIs and quantitative EEGs, in addition to neuropsych workups. Lindsey's results weren't a surprise; she showed clear signs of attention deficit problems, Miranda said. But he recommended a different medication than Ritalin.

But the other children's data yielded some surprises. Zach's tests showed signs of ADHD but also structural problems in his brain.

"He has an area of lack of development of the [hippocampus] here. This is a finding that explains some of the problems that he does have sometimes remembering or paying attention," Miranda said.

That information led Miranda to suggest not only medication but targeted therapy, in this case music lessons, to help teach the other side of Zach's brain to pick up the slack.

Miranda contends specialized memory exercises that appeal to one particular side of the brain can train it to take over for the slower side.

Megan showed no signs of attention deficits or other brain issues. Miranda suggested simply helping her with her reading. Without this puzzle piece Megan would likely have been put on medication. Mom had assumed that Megan, the youngest, likely had the same issue as her siblings.

Opening Up the Future

Having evidence behind what was happening to her kids was a comfort to Jensen. "You truly understand what you're looking at and what's going on in your kids' heads," she said. "And Dr. Miranda goes through each piece with you."

For Danny Rodgers, looking inside his head opened up his future.

When his grandmother, Jeanne, asked him what he wanted to do when he grew up, Danny replied earnestly, "Save the turtles, lower gas prices, and bring home the soldiers."

CHAPTER 2

Controversies About ADHD

ADHD Is a Real Medical Disorder

Stephen V. Faraone

In the following viewpoint Stephen V. Faraone contends that attention deficit hyperactivity disorder (ADHD) is a valid psychiatric diagnosis. Faraone does not think ADHD is the result of bad parenting or kids under stress. Faraone says psychiatrists use a set of criteria that was developed in 1970, to decide what constitutes a real and distinct psychiatric diagnosis. He says there is ample evidence to show that ADHD meets these criteria. He believes ADHD represents a valid psychiatric disorder separate from bipolar disorder, depression, or other psychiatric diagnoses and that it is important for physicians to understand the validity of the disorder in order to effectively treat their patients with ADHD. Stephen V. Faraone is a leading researcher in ADHD and a psychiatry professor in the psychiatry and behavioral sciences department and the neuroscience and physiology department at the State University of New York's Upstate Medical University.

Photo on facing page. While some psychiatrists contend that ADHD is a valid psychiatric diagnosis, others disagree. (© Images. com/Corbis)

SOURCE: Stephen V. Faraone, "The Scientific Foundation for Understanding Attention-Deficit/Hyperactivity Disorder as a Valid Psychiatric Disorder," *European Child and Adolescent Psychiatry,* vol. 14, 2005, pp. 1, 6–7. Copyright © 2005. Reproduced with kind permission from Springer Science and Business Media and the author.

For several decades, the mental health professions have recognized attention-deficit/hyperactivity disorder (ADHD) as a condition that affects 8–12% of children worldwide. Despite the high prevalence of the disorder and its widespread recognition among health professionals, the validity of the ADHD diagnosis has been challenged. Some claim that ADHD, rather than being a disorder, is an extreme of normal variation caused by normal childhood energy, boring classrooms, or overstressed parents and teachers. Others claim ADHD is caused by placing high demands on children and families to perform well in highly competitive environments. For these reasons, critics of the ADHD diagnosis argue against the psychopharmacologic treatment of the disorder and claim that stimulants—the most common psychopharmacologic therapy for ADHD—are overprescribed and unnecessary.

Media Have Created Uncertainties

In the scientific literature, the critics of ADHD are far outnumbered by those who view ADHD as a valid diagnosis, and clinical guidelines recognize ADHD as a valid and common psychiatric disorder of childhood. Yet, the popular media continue to place the minority opinion on an equal footing with the far greater majority. This has led to uncertainties among parents about whether to proceed with medical therapies and has further stigmatized affected families. As highlighted by a survey of pediatricians, parent and child misperceptions about ADHD and its treatment are common.

To clarify misconceptions about ADHD, clinicians need a framework for understanding and communicating that the science of psychiatry has rules of evidence for establishing the validity of disorders and that these rules have established ADHD as a valid psychiatric diagnosis. Knowledge of how the validity of ADHD has been established will be practically useful for clinicians who need to

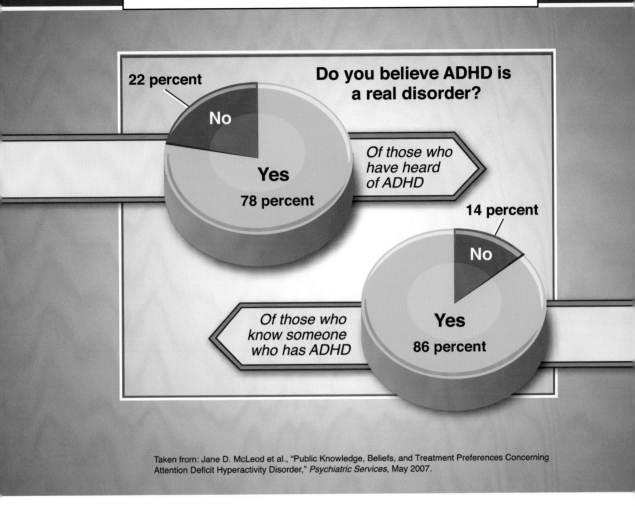

Do you believe ADHD is a real disorder?

22 percent

No

Yes
78 percent

Of those who have heard of ADHD

14 percent

No

Of those who know someone who has ADHD

Yes
86 percent

Taken from: Jane D. McLeod et al., "Public Knowledge, Beliefs, and Treatment Preferences Concerning Attention Deficit Hyperactivity Disorder," *Psychiatric Services*, May 2007.

help parents or colleagues understand these issues so that therapeutic choices can be based on the facts about the disorder rather than popular misconceptions.

Criteria to Determine the Validity of Psychiatric Diagnoses

[In 1970, psychiatrists Eli] Robins and [Samuel B.] Guze established a set of criteria for the validation of psychiatric diagnoses. Historically, the value of Robins and Guze's criteria was shown with the publication of the *Washington University Diagnostic Criteria*, from which *DSM-III*

[*Diagnostic and Statistical Manual of Mental Disorcders, 3rd edition*] and other empirical, structured criteria evolved. In their view, the validity of a diagnosis emerges from the converging evidence provided by many studies that examine the disorder from different perspectives. Robins and Guze developed their criteria at a time when American psychiatry was beginning two major changes. The field was abandoning the theory-bound diagnoses of the second edition of the American Psychiatric Association's *Diagnostic Manual (DSM-II)* for the empirically anchored diagnoses of the third edition *(DSM-III)* and was also undergoing a scientific revolution which increasingly recognized that much psychopathology could be explained by aberrant brain functioning. Due to these influences, Robins and Guze's criteria assert that the validity of any diagnosis must derive from empirical research and that some of this research must examine the neurobiologic causes and correlates of disorders.

FAST FACT

In statistics from 2004 through 2006, white children (9.8 percent) were more likely to have ADHD than black (8.6 percent) or Hispanic children (5.3 percent), according to the U.S. Centers for Disease Control and Prevention.

The Robins and Guze criteria view the validity of diagnoses as arising from empirical studies demonstrating the following: 1) the diagnosis has well-defined clinical correlates, 2) the diagnosis can be delimited from other diagnoses, 3) the disorder has a characteristic course and outcome, 4) the disorder shows evidence of heritability from family and genetic studies, 5) data from laboratory studies demonstrate other neurobiologic correlates of the disorder, and 6) the disorder shows a characteristic response to treatment. . . .

For clinicians who question the validity of the diagnosis of ADHD, [a review of the ways the Robins and Guze criteria apply to the diagnosis of ADHD] may resolve uncertainties by clarifying how the diagnosis satisfies the rules of evidence of scientific psychiatry. For other clinicians, understanding how their criteria apply to ADHD may have important clinical consequences. For the many clinicians who already accept the validity of ADHD, the Robins and Guze framework provides a useful tool for communicating complex information to parents and patients, information which, if understood, can improve treatment compliance and reduce stigma. . . .

ADHD Meets the Criteria

Extant [current or existing] studies provide ample evidence that ADHD meets the six Robins and Guze validity criteria as follows. 1) ADHD patients show a characteristic pattern of hyperactivity, inattention, and impulsivity that lead to adverse outcomes. 2) ADHD can be distinguished from other psychiatric disorders including those with which it is frequently comorbid. 3) Longitudinal studies show ADHD is not an episodic disorder. It is always chronic and it sometimes remits in adolescence or adulthood. When the disorder persists, so do its functional impairments. 4) Twin studies show ADHD is a highly heritable disorder, as heritable as schizophrenia or bipolar disorder. And molecular genetic studies have discovered genes that explain some of the disorder's genetic transmission. 5) Neuroimaging studies show that ADHD patients have abnormalities in the frontal-subcortical-cerebellar pathways involved in the control of attention, inhibition and motor behavior. 6) Most ADHD patients show a therapeutic response to medications that block the dopamine or norepinephrine transporter. . . .

Countering the Critics

Critics of the ADHD diagnosis would likely highlight several problems with the line of reasoning outlined in this paper. They might accept that a condition of high inattention, impulsivity and hyperactivity can be identified among children, but they view this as an extreme of normal variation, rather than a disorder. From this perspective, ADHD signs and symptoms are better viewed as a continuously varying trait (as we do personality) rather than evidence of a disorder. The problem with this view is its failure to recognize that even normal variation can become a disorder if extreme cases suffer from distress or disability. For example, although both blood pressure and serum cholesterol levels are continuously varying traits, that fact could not sensibly be used to argue that hypertension and hypercholesterolemia are not medically urgent disorders.

A reasonable counterargument to the genetic and neurobiologic findings about ADHD is that they are ir-

Psychiatrists use a set of criteria developed in 1970 to determine the characteristics of a particular psychiatric disorder. A majority of medical experts say that ADHD meets these criteria. **(Philippe Voisin/Photo Researchers, Inc.)**

relevant to the question of diagnostic validity because many "nondiagnostic" human traits are influenced by genes and by brain functioning. Red hair is a biological, genetic trait but not a disorder. This line of reasoning is flawed because it ignores a defining feature of the Robins and Guze approach, i.e., that diagnostic validity emerges from studies of all criteria, not from any single criterion. Red hair may be programmed by genes but it does not cause a pattern of distress or disability that would support it as a valid disorder. . . .

Those who discount the genetic and neurobiologic data might accept the existence of extreme and impairing ADHD symptoms but would argue that ADHD's impairments are due to the stresses of highly competitive societies, failures of parenting and teaching or societal intolerance of extreme but normal symptoms. Because twin studies show that environmental risk factors influence ADHD, it is possible that these social causes are relevant to the etiology of ADHD but firm conclusions must wait for systematic studies. For example, family studies suggest that adversity in the family environment is a risk factor for ADHD that cannot be explained by genetic transmission. This issue highlights a common misconception about Robins and Guze's biological perspective on the validation of diagnoses. The idea that the brain is the locus of a disorder's pathology does not repudiate the potential impact of environmental risk factors. In fact, as reviewed elsewhere, there is ample evidence that ADHD is a multifactorial disorder caused by the additive and interactive effects of genes and environmental risk factors.

Educating Patients and Parents About the Validity of ADHD

Inaccurate beliefs about the diagnostic validity of ADHD hinder the clinical care of the many ADHD patients and parents who have misgivings about seeking or accepting treatment. This suggests that an important part of management of the disorder is educating patients and parents about the nature of the disorder and the rationale for treatment. Education may be especially important in primary care settings because primary care practitioners such as pediatricians, family practice doctors, and internists are often the first health care professionals to hear about ADHD psychopathology from patients. Communicating accurate information about the disorder should encourage early treatment and limit the personal, family, and social burdens it causes.

ADHD Is Not a Real Medical Disorder

Sami Timimi and Nick Radcliffe

In the following viewpoint Sami Timimi and Nick Radcliffe contend that attention deficit hyperactivity disorder (ADHD) is not a valid medical disorder. Timimi and Radcliffe believe that ADHD is a "cultural construct" created by psychiatrists and facilitated by pharmaceutical companies. According to Timimi and Radcliffe, labeling kids as having ADHD is hostile toward children and prevents society from understanding them and their difficulties. Sami Timimi is a child and adolescent psychiatrist, and Nick Radcliffe is a clinical psychologist.

S omething strange has been happening to children in Western society in the past couple of decades. The diagnosis of Attention Deficit Hyperactivity Disorder (ADHD) has reached epidemic proportions, particularly amongst boys in North America. The diagnosis is usually made by a child psychiatrist or paediatrician

SOURCE: Sami Timimi and Nick Radcliffe, *Making and Breaking Children's Lives.* Ross-on-Wye, UK: PCCS Books, 2005. Copyright © Chapter 6: The Rise and Rise of ADHD by Sami Timimi and Nick Radcliffe. Reproduced by permission.

with advocates of the diagnosis claiming that children who present with what they consider to be over-activity, poor concentration and impulsivity are suffering from a medical condition which needs treatment with medication. The main medications used for children with a diagnosis of ADHD are stimulants such as Ritalin, whose chemical properties are virtually indistinguishable from the street drugs, speed and cocaine. Boys are four to ten times more likely to receive the diagnosis and stimulants than girls, with children as young as two being diagnosed and prescribed stimulants in increasing numbers.

By 1996 over 6 per cent of school-aged boys in America were taking stimulant medication with more recent surveys showing that in some schools in the United States over 17 per cent of boys have the diagnosis and are taking stimulant medication. In the UK [United Kingdom] prescriptions for stimulants have increased from about 6,000 in 1994 to about 345,000 in the latter half of 2003, suggesting that we in the UK are rapidly catching up with the US. Concerned professionals and parents are increasingly vocal in their criticism of the excessive use of stimulants and there are debates among clinicians proposing that ADHD is better regarded as a 'cultural construct' than a bona-fide medical disorder.

FAST FACT

The annual societal cost of ADHD was between $36 billion and $52 billion (in 2005 dollars), according to a 2007 estimate in the *Journal of Pediatric Psychology.*

Despite the assertion from ADHD industry insiders that 'ADHD' is a medical disorder, even they have to concede that despite years and millions of dollars spent on research (it is the most thoroughly researched child psychiatric label—from a biological perspective that is) no medical test for it exists, nor has any proof been forthcoming of what the supposed physical deficit is, and so diagnosis is based on the subjective opinion of the diagnoser. Indeed its validity as a distinct diagnostic entity is widely questioned as it cannot reliably be distinguished from other disorders in terms of aetiology [cause], course, cultural variation, response to treatment, co-morbidity [other diseases it appears with] and gender distribution. Furthermore there is no evidence that treatment with stimulants leads to any lasting improvement. Indeed a recent meta-analysis [a statistical analysis combining the results of several studies] of randomised controlled trials showed the trials were of poor quality, there was strong evidence of publication bias, short-term effects were inconsistent across different rating scales, side effects were frequent and problematic and long-term effects beyond four weeks of treatment were not demonstrated.

In the absence of objective methods for verifying the physical basis of ADHD, we also conceptualise ADHD as primarily a culturally constructed entity. The cultural dynamics of this label cannot be understood without first understanding the cultural discourses and power hierarchies that exist in contemporary Western society. It is a very compelling and dominating story invented and perpetuated by those whose interests are served by its telling and retelling (ADHD was literally voted into existence in the 1980s by the American Psychiatric Association when drawing up the third edition and third edition–revised versions of the *Diagnostic and Statistical Manual*). By focusing on within-child explanations for presenting behaviours, ADHD divorces a child from their context, and real life experiences, including traumatic ones, become clinically less important. In this article we explore how ADHD manages to occupy and hold onto such a dominant position despite the growing criticism and lack of evidence supporting its alleged medical origins.

The Claim That ADHD Is a Medical Disorder

To believers, ADHD is a diagnosable neuro-developmental disorder. Its identification is based on the observation of a constellation of behaviours that must be found across different settings and that are said to reveal abnormalities in children's activity levels, impulsiveness and concentration. Commonly, when a child is diagnosed the first-line treatment of choice is a stimulant such as Methylphenidate [Ritalin]. Stimulants are portrayed as safe and effective and children that are diagnosed and treated in this way are said to show vast improvements in their behaviour, activity levels, concentration and achievements. In the real world the picture is not so straightforward.

ADHD in Practice Is a Self-Fulfilling Process

In practice, the diagnosis of ADHD relies on adults in varying caring relationships with the child, reporting the above behaviours to a medical diagnostician. As diagnosis is based on the observation of behaviours alone, this has led to a kind of 'open season' where anyone can 'have a go': teachers, parents, school doctors, welfare officers, and so on. As the construct becomes more widely known within any community, confidence in making provisional diagnoses grows too. What is alarming is the apparent lack of awareness of the self-fulfilling nature of this process.

This self-fulfilling process occurs at many levels. For example, when a parent and child meet a specialist medical practitioner, the meeting is likely to be organised to elicit the type of information needed to fulfill predetermined diagnostic criteria. The relationship between the people's beliefs, expectations and subjective reporting will shape and inform the questions asked, responses given, and of course the child's behaviour in the room. Basically, some observable behaviours in children (such as inattention and hyperactivity) change in status from behaviours containing no more or less information (in isolation) than the inattention or hyperactivity as described by an observer, to becoming the basis of a primary diagnosis. The biomedical template is applied and the behaviours are interpreted as a sign of a physical disorder. This leaves out several layers of experience and context that could contribute to any observed behaviour as well as alternative meanings that could be given to that behaviour. This also denies the participant observers an opportunity to witness the child demonstrating exceptional behaviours. . . .

Behaviour rating scales have become a key part of the diagnostic process and are presented as an objective tool. Critics point out that agreeing on a cut-off point for the behaviours in question is a culturally and subjectively driven process which is reflected in the fact that epidemiological studies (using rating scales) have produced

Some clinicians argue that ADHD is not a valid medical disorder but rather a "cultural construct" created by psychiatrists and drug companies. (Phanie/ Photo Researchers, Inc.)

very different prevalence rates for ADHD (in its various forms), ranging from about 0.5 per cent of school age children to 26 per cent of school age children. The criteria used for rating behaviours are based on Likert-type frequency descriptors [a method of measuring attitudes] (for example, often, seldom, never, and so on), thus reliable diagnoses depend on how consistently raters share a common understanding of the behaviours to be rated. Despite attempts at standardising criteria and assessment tools in cross-cultural studies, major and significant differences between raters from different countries, as well as between raters from different ethnic minority backgrounds, continue to be apparent.

If trained professionals cannot agree on how to rate behaviours relative to some sort of agreed (all be it arbitrary) 'norm', it is not surprising that non-professional observers and informants have different thresholds. For example, [Professor Robert] Reid et al. cite several studies reporting that specialist teachers tend to be more tolerant of misbehaviour and judge students' behaviours as less deviant than general class teachers.

ADHD Is a Diagnostic "Dumping Ground"

ADHD is thus ideally placed as a convenient diagnostic 'dumping ground' allowing all of us (parents, teachers, doctors, politicians) to avoid the messy business of understanding human relationships and institutions and their difficulties, and our common responsibility for nurturing and raising well-behaved children. Loose, subjective diagnostic criteria with no established medical basis lend themselves to the 'elastic band' effect of ever stretching boundaries as the drug companies help themselves and the medical professions develop new markets. This has resulted in stimulants being prescribed for their perceived performance enhancing properties and with more children in classrooms taking stimulants many parents end up feeling their child is at a disadvantage if they do not. Stimulants are also being prescribed to children without them even fulfilling broad diagnostic criteria. This trend has now become so established that in some areas of the United States, less than half the children prescribed stimulants reach even the broad formal criteria for making a diagnosis of ADHD. In the UK you can now get a diagnosis via a 25-minute telephone consultation, without the child concerned being seen.

Why Is There Such a Strong Belief in ADHD?

ADHD exists as a concept because it has been positioned within the empiricist tradition of medical and psychological research. Writing on schizophrenia, [M.] Boyle draws attention to some of the devices that psychiatry uses to create the impression of a brain disorder despite the absence of supporting evidence. Firstly, she points out that by using their powerful status doctors can simply assert that it is a medical disorder in such a way as to minimise opposition. In the case of ADHD, the [Russell] Barkley et al. consensus statement[1] would be a good example of such rhetoric. Here a group of eminent psychiatrists and psychologists produced a consensus statement to forestall debate on the merits of the widespread diagnosis and drug treatment of ADHD. Secondly, to support the assertion of a medical disorder, apparently meaningful associations with biological processes are created. For example, funding research that supports claims of biological or genetic causes (whether this delivers results or not), leads to the construct implicitly being regarded as if it is part of a larger field (in the case of ADHD, neuro-developmental psychiatry). Thirdly, the medical discourse prevails by ignoring or rejecting other non-biological accounts of (in this case, children's)

[1] A statement signed by dozens of scientists claiming ADHD is a real medical disorder.

behaviour, or by co-opting them as peripheral or consequential rather than antecedent.

Privileged social groups, who hold important and influential positions, have a powerful effect on our common cultural beliefs, attitudes and practices. Child Psychiatry in the UK does appear to have re-invented itself in the last ten years. Having struggled with a crisis of identity about being doctors, influential child psychiatrists successfully influenced the UK's professional discourse convincing it that there were more personal rewards for the profession by it adopting a more medicalised American style approach: ADHD has, along with a string of other so-called disorders, helped construct the field of neuro-developmental psychiatry, which the public, trusting such high status opinions, has come to view as real.

Pharmaceutical Companies Contribute to Beliefs About ADHD

The development of diagnostic categories such as ADHD is of course of huge interest to the pharmaceutical industry. Indeed some argue that ADHD has been conceived and promoted by the pharmaceutical industry in order for there to be an entity for which stimulants could be prescribed. It is after all a multi-million dollar industry, with the US National Institute of Mental Health and the US Department of Education and the Food and Drug Administration all having been involved in funding and promoting treatment which calls for medicating children with behavioural problems. The situation with drug companies controlling the agenda of scientific debate has become so prevalent that it is virtually impossible to climb up the career ladder without promotional support from drug companies. Most senior academics have longstanding financial links with drug companies inevitably compromising the impartiality of their opinions.

Similarly the impartiality of patient support organisations has to be questioned. In recent years it has become apparent that drug companies are using such consumer lobbying groups to their advantage not only by (often secretly) generous donations, but also on occasion by setting up patient groups themselves. The main pro-medication pro-ADHD consumer support group in North America is CHADD [Children and Adults with Attention Deficit/Hyperactivity Disorder] which receives substantial amounts from drug companies, receiving an estimated $500,000 in 2002. There are other support groups: for example, in the United Kingdom the parent support group 'Overload' have been campaigning for prescribing doctors to provide more information to parents about the cardiovascular and neurological side effects of stimulants, believing that many more parents would be likely to reject such medication if they were being properly informed about it by the medical profession. However, without the financial support of the multinational giants, their message rarely gets heard.

ADHD is now also firmly entrenched in the cultural expectations of our education system. The defining of a disability requiring special needs help at school is now shaped by the disciplines of medicine and psychology. The adherence of these two fields to measuring physical and mental competence in order to determine normality inevitably conveys assumptions about deviance and failure and these labels then become attached to both individuals and groups who have failed to measure up or conform. Special needs practice in schools rests on within-child explanations. Psychiatric diagnoses have thus become an acceptable device for raising funds to meet children's perceived special needs. Increasing experience of children rendered less troublesome (to a school) by taking a stimulant, when coupled with a belief that these children's non-compliant behaviours were caused by a medical condition has also increased demand from teachers for children to be diagnosed and medicated.

The Effects of This New Category of Childhood

What are the effects of embracing practices that impose descriptions such as ADHD onto children's behaviour? Children quickly become objects of such descriptions. Their creativity, capacity for 'exceptional behaviours' and diversity go unnoticed. ADHD pushes teachers, parents and medical practitioners into self-doubt about their capacity to teach and care for children. The opportunities for developing reflexive, appreciative child management practices and skills are lost.

In mental health settings, the chance to build a repertoire of therapeutic skills and practices that might facilitate people to talk about their experience in ways that can create more empowering meanings that build on their own knowledge is also lost. Instead children are persuaded to take highly addictive and potentially brain disabling drugs for many years and may well be cultured into the attitude of 'a pill for life's problems'. Children and their carers risk developing 'tunnel vision' about their problems rendering them unnecessarily 'disabled' and dependent on 'experts'. The effect this has not only on the physical health of our children in the West, but also on our ways of viewing childhood is incalculable. Behind the rise in diagnoses and the liberal prescription of such dangerous medicines lurks a deep malaise that is infecting Western culture—hostility to children—for in our modernist, hyperactive, individualistic lifestyles children 'get in the way'.

ADHD Is Underdiagnosed and Undertreated

William Dodson

In the following viewpoint William Dodson maintains that most people who have attention deficit hyperactivity disorder (ADHD) are undiagnosed and untreated. Dodson discusses the scientific basis for ADHD and the effectiveness of medication to treat it. According to Dodson, studies indicate that ADHD is more common than prevalence rates indicate, and a large proportion of people diagnosed with ADHD do not receive medication or any other kind of treatment. William Dodson is a psychiatrist in Denver, Colorado.

The scientific understanding of Attention Deficit Hyperactivity Disorder (ADHD) has probably made more progress in the last five years than it did in all the years since it was first described in 1937. Until recently, almost all of our information about ADHD was based on studies of *hyperactive* elementary school–aged boys. We still know very little about adults

SOURCE: William Dodson, "ADHD: The Basics and the Controversies," *Understanding Our Gifted*, Summer 2002. Reproduced by permission.

with ADHD or about females at any age. It has only been the last few years, as these children have grown into adulthood and started their own families, that a more complete longitudinal [long-term] picture has begun to emerge and the far ranging effects of the disorder appreciated.

[In 1998 in] response to the concerted disinformation campaign waged by the Church of Scientology, the American Medical Association (AMA) issued a Council Report in an effort to get accurate information to people with the condition, their families, their physicians, and their teachers. . . . The AMA asked and then answered six basic questions about ADHD.

The Existence of ADHD

1. Does ADHD really exist or is it, as alleged by the Church of Scientology, a myth? One of the outcomes of answering the disinformation about ADHD for more than a decade is that now ADHD is "one of the best researched disorders in medicine, and the overall data on its validity are far more compelling than for many medical conditions" [according to L.S. Goldman].

ADHD is the classic neuropsychiatric disorder—that is, a brain-based disorder with a primarily behavioral presentation. ADHD has a strong genetic clustering (80 percent), but its etiology [cause] is unknown. Like all other developmental disabilities, ADHD is a lifelong condition. Its manifestations and the patient's compensation to the disorder change throughout the lifespan. The basic features, impairments, and treatments, however, are very similar for both children and adults. People do not "outgrow" ADHD, just as no one outgrows any other genetic or developmental disorder. All people develop better abilities to pay attention and control impulses as they grow older. Most patients will benefit from lifelong medication, even if they have "learned to cope," because life stresses increase rather than diminish with age.

We once indulged in the wishful thinking that ADHD usually disappeared in adolescence. What we were actually seeing was the transformation of the most visible feature of bounce-off-the-wall hyperactivity into mere restlessness.

The disorder is manifested as a persistent pattern of inattention, easy distractibility and/or hyperactivity-impulsivity that is significantly more severe than that observed in persons of a comparable level of development. This inattention and/or impulsivity interfere significantly in all areas of function (school, work, social/family relationships, mood regulation, and self-esteem). In identified cases the gender ratio is 3:1, male to female, through adolescence but approaches almost 1:1 in adults.

Attention "Deficit," however, is a terrible name. Most people with ADHD report that their attention is not deficit, it is excessive. People with ADHD describe that they are drawn to all the stimuli around them equally and simultaneously. They are like jugglers who give fleeting attention to each ball in the air. Nothing gets sustained, undivided involvement.

For persons with ADHD, the ability to maintain attention and impulse control is determined by one factor—if the task is interesting, desired, or challenging, the individual with ADHD has no problem with distractibility or impulsivity. If, on the other hand, the task is boring, it is a neurologic impossibility to stay on task. Interest and challenge only determine the ability to function, not importance. This "interest based performance" is coming to be the hallmark diagnostic symptom of the disorder and the key to successful management once medication treatment has been established.

The swings of attention can be profound from states of "zoned out" dissociation to a condition known as *hyperfocus*. As many as 40 percent of adolescents and adults with ADHD can enter what appears to be an altered state of consciousness while doing activities which they consider particularly intriguing. During a hyperfocus the person performs at almost 100 percent efficiency, does not notice the passage of time, does not become tired or hungry, and has virtually 100 percent comprehension and retention of what he reads.

This inconsistency of performance based on interest leaves the impression that the ability to function is under the control of the ADHD patient who is just being lazy or uncooperative. We used to use a trick question with the parents of children brought in for assessment of ADHD. We asked them what their child's favorite TV program was in the smug belief that a truly ADHD child would not sit long enough to have a favorite program. Now we understand that more than half of children and adults have the ability to become deeply and productively involved in tasks that interest and challenge them, only to fall apart when they become bored.

FAST FACT

According to a 2006 study in the *Journal of American College Health*, more college students take stimulants illicitly (5.4 percent) than take them for medical use (2.2 percent).

Many people would also like to drop the term "disorder" because ADHD seems to convey a large number of positive traits along with the distractibility and impulsivity. People with ADHD usually have much higher than average intelligence, although they commonly express frustration at not being able to demonstrate it consistently. They tend to be very creative and inventive. Sometimes this presents as being artistic, musical, or inventive, but almost always it manifests itself in intuitive problem solving. People with ADHD can often pull together the threads in complex problems to develop ingenious solutions that no one else would ever see. People with ADHD are also described as having "relentless determination" whenever they do hook into a challenge. Finally, people with ADHD tend to be affable, likable people who often have a quick and zany sense of humor. They tend to have a close, tight group of friends and family who describe them as being "high maintenance but high reward" individuals.

The Prevalence of ADHD

2. How common is ADHD and what accounts for its being diagnosed more often in the United States? There is a misperception that ADHD is a diagnosis of white, middle class, American boys. In fact, every time that prevalence studies have been done around the world, ADHD has been found in much the same rates. It has not mattered whether it was New Zealand, Puerto Rico, China, England, or Germany. Rather than being an American disorder, ADHD seems to be something that is fundamentally human and present if one bothers to look for it.

The historic estimates for prevalence are almost certainly low at 3 to 5 percent of the population because only the hyperactive or "noisy" child was detected, and the "silent," purely inattentive child was missed. Two recent, nearly identical prospective studies give clearer estimates indicating that ADHD may be more common than major depression, bipolar mood disorder, schizophrenia, panic disorder, and obsessive-compulsive disorder *combined*. If these estimates are correct, ADHD is not "over-diagnosed" or a fad diagnosis. Three out of four people with the disorder still go undetected.

Adverse Effects of ADHD

3. What are the adverse consequences of having ADHD that would justify its treatment? By definition, in order to make the diagnosis of ADHD, the person has to have significant impairment in at least two areas of functioning. In real life this is usually easy to do since ADHD impairs every area of life. For example:

1. Accidents are the leading cause of death until the age of 44. Without treatment, adolescents with ADHD have 400 percent more serious injuries and 300 percent

more motor vehicle violations than do adolescents without ADHD or adolescents with ADHD who consistently take medication.

2. Perhaps the primary historical focus of outcome research has been on academic functioning. Despite more than adequate intellectual ability, adolescents with ADHD are three times more likely to have failed one or more grades, been suspended, or expelled. Eighty percent of persons who drop out of school before attaining a high school diploma have ADHD, an impairing learning disability, or both.

3. Many people with ADHD try to self-medicate their illness. Until the age of 15, drug and alcohol experimentation is little different from non-ADHD adolescents. After age 15, however, the risk of a substance use diagnosis triples as compared to the general population. Luckily, treatment with stimulant class medication seems to protect against this increased risk.

4. In the longest longitudinal outcome study thus far done, [psychiatrist Russell] Barkley (1996) has followed a cohort of ADHD children into their mid-20s. Their sexual lives give a grim look at the impact of untreated ADHD. At the most recent follow-up more than half of the ADHD group had been tested for HIV disease. No one in the matched control group had been tested. Of the 43 children born to participants in the study, 42 had been born to the ADHD group. Perhaps the most disturbing finding was that 54 percent of these parents had already lost custody of their children.

ADHD impairs every aspect of life, and the consequences of not treating ADHD get worse as the individual gets older. Car accidents are worse than scrapes on the playground; losing a job that supports your family is worse than having to repeat the 2nd grade; alcoholism is worse than eating candy to slow down. Strong consideration

should be given to treatment in every case and earlier rather than later before:

- the individual falls behind academically and loses hope of ever catching up.
- the aggressive/disruptive behavior interferes with the parent-child bond.
- the behavior gets the person labeled as a "bad kid."
- the children label themselves as lazy, stupid, and "bad."

When children with ADHD enter adolescence, they may be three times more likely to have failed one or more grades or to have been suspended or expelled from school. (© Butch Martin/Alamy)

Treatment for ADHD

4. What, then, is the best treatment for ADHD? Here the AMA came down very strongly on the fact that there are more than 170 double blind, controlled studies which demonstrate that the mild stimulant medications were the best studied, most effective, best tolerated, and safest treatment of ADHD.

Since the Council Report was issued, another important study of the treatment of ADHD has been published. The Multimodal Treatment Study of ADHD, or "MTA," is the largest and longest study of a mental disorder in children ever done. It was designed to answer once and for all what is the optimal treatment for ADHD.

The 579 children in the study were selected because they had "screaming ADHD" that was unmistakable. These children were randomly divided into four treatment groups:

1. Just stimulant class medication that was fine-tuned to the needs of each unique child
2. Just intensive behavior management
3. Both medication and intensive behavior management
4. A community treatment group to see what was happening in the real world

At the end of 24 months the results were striking. The two groups that received medication did exceptionally well. The group that got both medication and intensive behavioral therapy did no better than the children who received only medication. The group that got behavioral treatment alone did improve but much less than those who received medication. Surprisingly, when the follow-up assessments were done three months after the intensive behavioral therapy had ended, no evidence could be found that the therapy had ever occurred. Just as with medication treatment, when the behavioral treatment ended, so did the benefits. This also was consistent with what was so commonly seen in the real world . . . families would become hyper-structured in order to help an ADHD child succeed, but the child would flounder as soon as she left the family to try to make it out in the real world that was not structured for her. The group that did by far the worst was the community treatment group.

Out in their communities one third of these children with "screaming ADHD" received no treatment of any kind, and those that did were significantly *under-dosed* when given medication. As with the other studies that came before, the MTA demonstrated that the assertion that ADHD is over-diagnosed and over-treated has no basis whatsoever in fact.

It is important to be very specific about what the MTA means and doesn't mean.

It DOES NOT mean that adjunctive treatments such as behavioral management are not effective or not needed. These treatments are often absolutely necessary to teach the self control and social consciousness that were not learned at age appropriate times due to the interference of ADHD. Behavior management and "trying harder" do not treat the major criteria of inattention, impulsivity, and motor restlessness.

It DOES mean that:

1. ADHD is not the result of bad parenting skills. These were good, involved parents who got even better. It just didn't make any difference.

2. ADHD is not the result of a defect in character or laziness. Trying harder even with the intensive support of specialists in the field was ineffective.

3. Stimulant medications are where everyone should start, not the treatment of last resort when everything else has failed. Therefore, start medication as early as possible before maladaptive coping mechanisms and self-image issues become ingrained.

4. "Pills don't give skills." Medication levels the neurologic playing fields so that the many needed remedial interventions have a hope of being effective. Once the ADHD is under consistent control, many other interventions are often necessary and beneficial. Children and adults need remedial education to make up for the classroom work to which they could not pay

attention. They need to learn organization and time management skills. They need to learn how to interpret non-verbal social cues and how to understand the emotions of others. They must learn how to understand their own emotional states and intimate relationships. The medication "gets them into the game" with a realistic hope of success.

The Consequences of Medications

5. What are the adverse consequences of using the stimulant class of medications to treat ADHD? Once again the AMA emphasized that the minor stimulants were both safe and well tolerated if properly taken, stating that, "Adverse effects from stimulants are generally mild, short lived, and responsive to dosing or timing adjustments." They acknowledged that in the early years of medication treatment of ADHD, many patients had been prescribed higher dosages than necessary in the mistaken belief that "more medication is better." We now know that the dose of medication that provides optimal performance and benefits has no side effects except a mild, transient loss of appetite. Unfortunately, no one can predict the dose of medication that produces optimal performance based on any known parameter. . . .

- Not severity of the disorder
- Not body weight or height
- Not age
- Not gender
- Not baseline scores from any rating scale or continuous performance test

Everyone must fine-tune the dose of medication to his or her unique needs and biochemistry.

Thus far, ALL of the adverse consequences are associated with NOT treating the disorder. There was initially some concern that treatment with mild stimulants in childhood might predispose some children to drug abuse in later life. Recent research has demonstrated that exactly the opposite is true.

Appropriate Assessments

6. Are children being appropriately assessed or is ADHD being overdiagnosed? Every time that Congress has asked the [National Institute of Mental Health, part of the] National Institutes of Health (NIMH) to investigate these

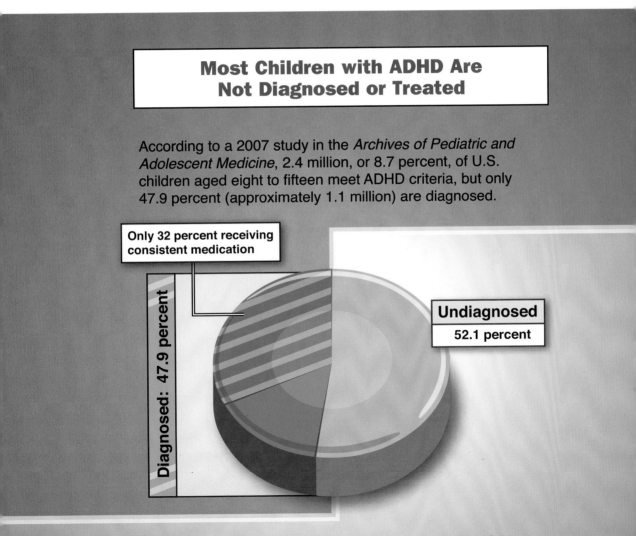

Most Children with ADHD Are Not Diagnosed or Treated

According to a 2007 study in the *Archives of Pediatric and Adolescent Medicine*, 2.4 million, or 8.7 percent, of U.S. children aged eight to fifteen meet ADHD criteria, but only 47.9 percent (approximately 1.1 million) are diagnosed.

Only 32 percent receiving consistent medication

Diagnosed: 47.9 percent

Undiagnosed

52.1 percent

Taken from: Tanya E. Froehlich et al., "Prevalence, Recognition, and Treatment of Attention Deficit Hyperactivity Disorder in a National Sample of U.S. Children," *Archives of Pediatric and Adolescent Medicine*, September 2007.

concerns, we have found that the majority of people with ADHD are never detected and offered treatment. The MTA study demonstrated that one-third of the children referred into their communities with documented "screaming ADHD" got no services whatsoever. Those who did receive some form of intervention usually got medication, but, at doses that were on average half of what the study had determined to be optimal doses. An NIMH study by [psychiatrist Peter] Jensen (1999) of the patterns of treatment in all mental disorders in children found that only one in eight children with ADHD had received services of any kind (school intervention/medication, behavioral treatment, social skills training, etc.) in the previous 12 months. Increased recognition (especially in girls) and increased willingness to treat ADHD has made it seem that there has been an explosion of the disorder in recent years. The irony is that despite a tremendous increase in our awareness of ADHD, all of the evidence points to the fact that it is still grossly under-diagnosed and under-treated.

ADHD is here to stay. It is neither a myth nor an over-reaction. It is a genetically based condition that usually presents in childhood but continues to impair life functioning throughout the life cycle. It has a good, safe, and effective treatment with a combination of stimulant class medications and skill building. When aggressively treated early, the disorder does not continue to invisibly hold back the people who have the condition, and they can go on to have happy and productive lives.

ADHD Is Overdiagnosed and ADHD Medications Are Overprescribed

Tom Glaister

In the following viewpoint Tom Glaister asserts that kids in the United States are being overdiagnosed as having attention defict hyperactivity disorder (ADHD) and are being overmedicated with Ritalin, a drug that resembles speed and has significant side effects. Glaister suggests that most of the kids being diagnosed with ADHD probably do not really have the disorder. If kids are hyperactive, says Glaister, it is not because they have a genetic disorder. It is probably because society has become increasingly technological and fast paced, and because parents are not paying enough attention to their children. Glaister thinks it is wrong to give potentially dangerous drugs to children. Tom Glaister is a correspondent for *Consumer Affairs*, a consumer-oriented magazine.

T he first time I heard of Ritalin was when I was volunteering as a teenager, teaching math at home to a single mother who was trying to get her high school diploma.

SOURCE: Tom Glaister, "Doping the Young: The ADHD Dilemma," www.consumeraffairs.com, November 12, 2007. Reproduced by permission.

As we struggled our way through fractions and percentages, I had to duck as a tea cup came flying through the air and smashed against the wall behind me—her 4-year-old son, Jan, had woken up and wanted some attention. Much wailing and screaming and sounds of heavy crashes later, my student came back down the stairs having put her son to bed.

"I don't get a minute of peace," she sobbed. "He just never stops. Sometimes the kindergarten even calls me up to bring him back home when he gets too disruptive."

Ritalin Is Proposed as the ADHD Solution

The solution, the doctors told her, was to give him a daily dose of Ritalin, a drug with a similar structure to amphetamines. She didn't understand how giving 'speed' to her child was going to slow him down but it seemed to help and she felt like she'd run out of options.

We all remember the problem kid in the school classroom. The one who could never sit still, kept pulling the girls' hair and forgot the teacher's instructions within minutes. They used to call kids like that trouble makers or just plain dumb. They got low grades, a bad reputation and often dropped out of school early, much to everyone's relief.

Now, thanks to masses of genetic and behavioral research, most of these kids are classified as ADHD (Attention-Deficit Hyperactivity Disorder) or, if they're unable to concentrate but in a non-disruptive kind of way, plain old ADD [attention deficit disorder].

As every fashionable psychological condition is inevitably accompanied with a heavily-marketed drug to treat it, the last 20 years have seen Ritalin becoming a household name in America. Drug companies, doctors and schools across the country have pushed the drug so much that now around 5 million American children daily pop the pill to help them concentrate.

Ritalin Seemed Like a Godsend

For overworked teachers in schools, Ritalin seemed like a godsend. The problem kids began to listen, behave and let the rest of the class learn. Schools even began to ask parents of disruptive children to get them on Ritalin or one of its close relatives as soon as possible.

If not, they argued, the child would be unable to learn, become more rebellious and anti-social with the years and the statistics, after all, show that young offenders frequently suffer from ADHD. If only they'd been treated in time. . . .

ADHD not only became all the rage for children but many adults, too, found a new lease in life in explaining why they find it hard to concentrate. It's genetic, you see. Give them some drugs and they'll be able to focus on the task in hand and get their life together.

I met a medical student who was on Ritalin and he declared it was vital to his college education. Without it he just couldn't study for more than about 5 hours at a time. When I suggested that 5 hours of memorizing long lists of symptoms and conditions might already be asking too much of himself, he looked at me like I was nuts.

Hyperactivity and low attention spans are a reality, no doubt about it. Families suffer all over America because of uncontrollable children running wild.

Something Is Badly Wrong

But a social phenomenon doesn't necessarily translate into a genetic brain disorder—at least not one that has to be treated with addictive drugs. When 5 million children are fed pills in order to function in a classroom setting, it seems something is badly wrong.

When I was a child the teachers complained that I was always daydreaming. I lived in a fantasy world of my own and paid little attention to what was written on the board. I didn't complete the assignments and was kept in during breaks until the teacher finally just gave up.

Some medical experts say that psychiatrists are too quick to prescribe Ritalin and other drugs to children diagnosed with ADHD. (Steve Liss/Time Life Pictures/Getty Images)

Had I been born 20 years later, I would probably have been diagnosed with ADD and stuffed with Ritalin to help me focus.

But I didn't need drugs. The reason I didn't concentrate was that my parents were splitting up and I found the lessons boring beyond belief. With schools on a tight schedule and an even tighter budget, however, it's far easier to just blame it all on the genes and recommend medication.

As Robert Reid of the University of Nebraska noted: "The allure of ADHD is that it is 'a label of forgiveness.' The kid's problems are not his parents' fault, not the teacher's fault, not the kid's fault. It's better to say this kid has ADHD than to say this kid drives everybody up the wall. But to really work out what's going on would mean psychological profiling and that would take time and money."

Slow Hands

I remember in school how the better part of my attention was focused on the clock on the wall, willing the hands to move around faster to the final bell of freedom. It was only years later when I got my first job that I realized that this regimentation was training for the working life that lay ahead for most of us.

Fortunately, in the world of work it's not necessary to be the kind of person who can [sit] still for 8 hours a day. If you have ADHD symptoms of excess energy you might make an excellent bartender, salesman or entrepreneur.

After all, the world is better off because humans are of such varied natures and talents—we'd hardly expect the same qualities of an acrobat as an accountant.

Most schools, on the other hand, are structured as though children were all the same. There simply aren't enough resources to customize the education of each child to their needs and strengths. The structure of the curriculum and the school day is designed to meet the needs of the average student at the expense of the kids for whom such a system just won't work. Unless they're drugged.

Where Did ADHD Come From?

But where does ADHD come from? Have there always been millions of American kids who couldn't concentrate or is it a modern disease?

It seems that most current scientific thinking holds ADHD to be largely a genetic syndrome. Studies indicate that it's passed on from parents to their children and there seem to be noticeable differences in the brains of ADHD and ADD children.

The same can of course be said for Buddhist monks that meditate a lot and professional musicians, but I'm not a neurologist and so I won't go there.

In fact, there's rarely much room to argue with the scientists. They're specialists in their fields, the evidence always looks overwhelming and in any case, tens of millions of dollars of drug sales depend on them being right.

What we can do is observe some of the changes in the culture over the last 50 years and ask ourselves if the condition that we observe in hyperactive kids might actually be a syndrome?

In my travels around the world I've been fortunate enough to see how children grow up in less modern countries. In most places, children still play together in the street and their parents aren't afraid they'll be abducted.

They return home to a large extended family and the responsibility for feeding, nurturing and entertaining the child is taken by whichever uncle, sister or grandmother happens to be around at the time.

Didn't it used to be like that in America, too?

In developed countries, however, it's often considered too dangerous for children to play outside on their own, so they immerse themselves in television or computer games and, as people live increasingly alone, it's up to the overworked, stressed parents to shoulder the entire burden of raising them. It brings to mind a quote from *The Simpsons* when Bart tells Homer: "It's just hard not to listen to TV: it's spent so much more time raising us than you have."

Parental Attention Deficit

Maybe some of the children on Ritalin are indeed suffering from a deficiency of attention in that they never received enough—attention from their families, that is.

As for the adults, ADD may be symptomatic of the world we live in rather than a genetic condition. Why is it, for example, that in spite of all the wonderful time-saving devices that we have invented—the washing machine, the cell phone, the car—that we never actually have any time?

And that's not to mention the age of technology addiction. In a society where you can be reached at any time, distraction has forced its way into our lives.

The intimate conversation interrupted by the ringing of a cell phone. Waking up in the morning and checking your email before washing your face. If attention is something that you have to pay it's little wonder that so many of us are broke.

In the bestseller, *Driven to Distraction*, Edward Hallowell and John Ratey reason that: "American society tends to create ADD-like symptoms in us all. The fast pace. The sound bite. The quick cuts. The TV remote-control clicker. It is important to keep this in mind, or you may start thinking that everybody you know has ADD."

Ok, so this is still speculative. But so was the observation known to just about any parent that their children get hyper after consuming too much soda and candy. Until recently science wrote off the alarm about artificial colors and additives as hippie nonsense. However, that all changed when a British study group recently published a paper in the *Lancet*, concluding that: "The finding lends strong support for the case that food additives exacerbate hyperactive behaviors (inattention, impulsivity and overactivity) at least into middle childhood."

Is giving your child Ritalin the price of a lousy diet?

Here's a little known gem: Novartis, the pharmaceutical company that makes Ritalin, owned until [2007] Gerber Products Company. Get that? The company that sells drugs for hyperactive children also used to sell baby food, a product containing additives that might in themselves cause hyperactivity. One hell of a way to create a market.

The ADHD Bandwagon

Of course, at the end of the day, Ritalin does work. But if a child appears to 'improve' on medication it doesn't mean that the diagnosis was accurate. Drugs with the

> **FAST FACT**
>
> According to national health statistics, 4.3 percent of American children are being treated for ADHD with medications such as Adderall, Ritalin, or Strattera.

effect of amphetamines make everyone focus. That's why armies give them out to their soldiers in the field.

Trouble is, like most drugs they have side effects, causing problems with appetite, amnesia, possibly problems with growth glands and sometimes cardiovascular difficulties. Indeed, the deaths of 25 patients, 19 of them children, prompted the FDA [Food and Drug Administration] last year [2006] to demand a black box warning for Ritalin, Concerta and other legal stimulant drugs.

All of this doesn't say that ADHD doesn't exist—I've only to think of little Jan aiming a teacup at my head to believe it—but the current bandwagon of slapping brain

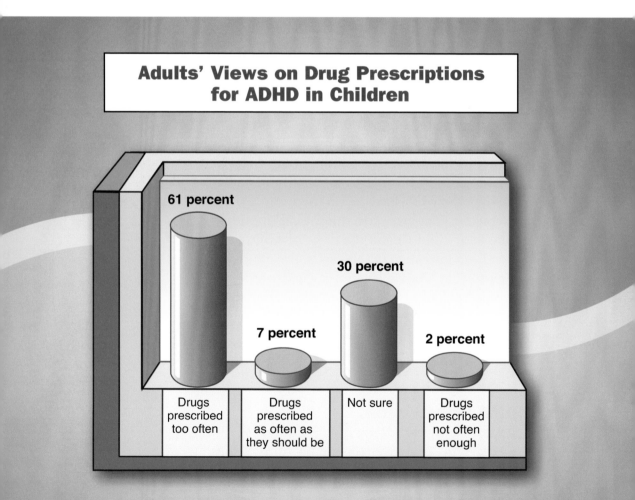

Adults' Views on Drug Prescriptions for ADHD in Children

61 percent — Drugs prescribed too often

7 percent — Drugs prescribed as often as they should be

30 percent — Not sure

2 percent — Drugs prescribed not often enough

Taken from: Joyce Frieden, "Most Adults Think ADHD Drugs Are Overprescribed," *Pediatric News*, July 2006/*Wall Street Journal* Online/Harris Interactive.

disorder labels on troubled children is out of control. For one thing, it can become a self-fulfilling prophecy where a child learns he needs drugs in order to fit in. Granted, that might make him a customer of psychotropic medication for life but does little to help him understand himself.

Drugs Handed Out So Casually

Adults are old enough to decide if they want to take medication. If Ritalin helps them get through their day, they at least have the maturity to decide for themselves. But when social workers put pressure on parents to take out prescriptions for their children and school nurses spend more time administering drugs than anything else, we've reached a state of affairs where the 'war on drugs' was lost long ago.

In fact, Ritalin has taken youth drug culture by storm and is sometimes known as 'poor man's cocaine'. Tablets are swallowed or crushed up and snorted, sometimes for the high or sometimes as an appetite-suppressant by weight-conscious teens.

If drugs are to be handed out casually and liberally by health care professionals, it's not surprising that juveniles should treat recreational use of the same with the same blasé attitude.

Alternative Therapies May Be Useful in Treating ADHD

Tara Parker-Pope

In the following viewpoint Tara Parker-Pope contends that concerns about the side effects of drugs for attention deficit hyperactivity disorder (ADHD) are causing many people to look to alternative treatments, such as herbal remedies and dietary modifications. Some studies have suggested that omega-3 fatty acid supplements might help ease ADHD symptoms, and other studies indicate that artificial food colorings and preservatives may exacerbate the hyperactive behaviors of patients with ADHD. Tara Parker-Pope has written about health issues for The New York Times, The Wall Street Journal, *and* The Houston Chronicle.

About 2.5 million children in the United States take stimulant drugs for attention and hyperactivity problems. But concerns about side effects have prompted many parents to look elsewhere: as many as two-thirds of children with attention deficit hyperactivity

SOURCE: Tara Parker-Pope, "Weighing Nondrug Options for ADHD," *New York Times,* June 17, 2008. Reproduced by permission.

disorder, or A.D.H.D., have used some form of alternative treatment.

The most common strategy involves diet changes, like giving up processed foods, sugars and food additives. About 20 percent of children with the disorder have been given some form of herbal therapy; others have tried supplements like vitamins and fish oil or have used biofeedback, massage and yoga.

Drugs Are Not Always an Option

While some studies of alternative treatments show promise, there is little solid research to guide parents. That is unfortunate, because for some children, prescription drugs aren't an option.

The drugs have been life-changing for many children. But nearly one-third experience worrisome side effects, and a 2001 report in *The Canadian Medical Association Journal* found that for more than 10 percent, the effects could be severe—including decreased appetite and weight loss, insomnia, abdominal pain and personality changes.

Although the drugs are widely viewed as safe, many parents were alarmed when the Food and Drug Administration ordered in 2006 that stimulants like Adderall, Ritalin and Concerta carry warnings of risk for sudden death, heart attacks and hallucinations in some patients.

Hope for Herbal Remedies

What about the alternatives? [In June 2008], *The Journal of the American Medical Association* reported that the first study of the herb St. John's wort worked no better than a placebo to counter A.D.H.D. But the trial, of 54 children, lasted only eight weeks, and even prescription drugs can take up to three months to show a measurable effect.

But the larger issue may be that in complementary medicine, one treatment is rarely used alone, making the range of alternative remedies difficult to study. Natural treatments may well be beneficial, said the report's lead

In 2001 a study of the use of the herb ginkgo biloba to treat ADHD, children showed improvement after four weeks. (Kathy Merrifield/Photo Researchers, Inc.)

author, Wendy Weber, a research associate professor at the school of naturopathic medicine at Bastyr University in Kenmore, Wash. "We just need to do more studies and document the effect."

Other herbal treatments for the disorder include echinacea, ginkgo biloba and ginseng. There are no reliable data on echinacea; a 2001 study showed improvement after four weeks in children using ginkgo and ginseng, but there was no control group for comparison.

There is more hope for omega-3 fatty acids, found in fish and fish-oil supplements. A review [in 2007] in the journal *Pediatric Clinics of North America* concluded that a "growing body of evidence" supported the use of such supplements for children with A.D.H.D.

Dietary Modification

As for dietary changes, a 2007 study in *The Lancet* examined the effect of artificial coloring and preservatives on hyperactive behavior in children. After consuming an additive-free diet for six weeks, the children were given either a placebo beverage or one containing a mix of additives in two-week intervals. In the additive group, hyperactive behaviors increased.

The study caused many pediatricians to rethink their skepticism about a link between diet and A.D.H.D. "The overall findings of the study are clear and require that even we skeptics, who have long doubted parental claims of the effects of various foods on the behavior of their children, admit we might have been wrong," reported a February issue of *AAP Grand Rounds*, a publication of the American Academy of Pediatrics.

Data on sugar avoidance are less persuasive. Several studies suggest that any link between sugar and hyperactivity is one of parental perception, rather than reality. In one study, mothers who were told the child received sugar reported more hyperactive behavior, even when the food was in fact artificially sweetened. Mothers who were told the child received a low-sugar snack were less likely to report worse behavior.

Biofeedback Therapy

One interesting option is a form of biofeedback therapy in which children wear electrodes on their head and learn to control video games by exercising the parts of the brain related to attention and focus. Research has suggested that the method works just as well as medication, and many children report that they enjoy it.

The challenge is finding a doctor who will help explore the range of options. For instance, the best way to tell whether dietary changes may help is to eliminate the foods and then reintroduce them, monitoring the child's behavior all the while. The best evidence may come from a teacher who is unaware of any change in diet.

> **FAST FACT**
>
> An estimated 7,873 drug-related emergency department visits involved either methylphenidate or amphetamine-dextroamphetamine, the two most commonly prescribed medications for ADHD, according to the Substance Abuse and Mental Health Services Administration's Drug Abuse Warning Network for 2004.

Use of Complementary and Alternative Medicine (CAM) to Treat ADHD

46 percent of parents surveyed did not use CAM therapies to treat their child's ADHD

54 percent of parents surveyed used CAM therapies, including vitamins and dietary manipulation, to treat their child's ADHD

Taken from: Eugenia Chan et al., "Complementary and Alternative Therapies in Childhood Attention and Hyperactivity Problems," *Journal of Developmental and Behavioral Pediatrics*, February 2003.

A Holistic Approach

The Integrative Pediatrics Council . . . offers a list of pediatricians who offer alternative treatments. Its chairman, Dr. Lawrence D. Rosen, chief of pediatric integrative medicine at Hackensack University Medical Center in New Jersey, says parents should seek a holistic approach. But he notes that that may well include prescription drugs.

"I do prescribe medications in my practice, and there are kids whose lives have been saved by that," he said. "But it's a holistic approach that is very different than one pill, one symptom. We're addressing not just the physical, chemical needs of kids, but their total emotional and mental health."

Children Should Undergo Heart Screening Before Taking Stimulants to Treat ADHD

D. Woodrow Benson and Christena H. Benson

In the following viewpoint D. Woodrow Benson and Christena H. Benson discuss the reasons behind the recommendation of the American Heart Association (AHA) that children should receive electrocardiograms (ECGs) before being prescribed stimulants to treat attention deficit hyperactivity disorder (ADHD). The authors say that there are concerns that stimulants, which increase heart rate and blood pressure, can cause sudden cardiac death in some children and adolescents. They say more studies need to be done to quantify these risks, but performing ECGs, as the AHA recommends, can be useful. D. Woodrow Benson is a physician and Christena H. Benson is a registered nurse at Cincinnati Children's Hospital Medical Center.

Attention deficit hyperactivity disorder (ADHD) is estimated to affect 4% to 5% of the pediatric population, but the prevalence may be higher in children with heart disease. Numerous studies have identified that ADHD has substantial morbidity, including

SOURCE: D. Woodrow Benson and Christena H. Benson, "Stimulant Medications in Children and Adolescents: A Big Problem for Little People?" *Circulation*, April 22, 2008. Reproduced by permission.

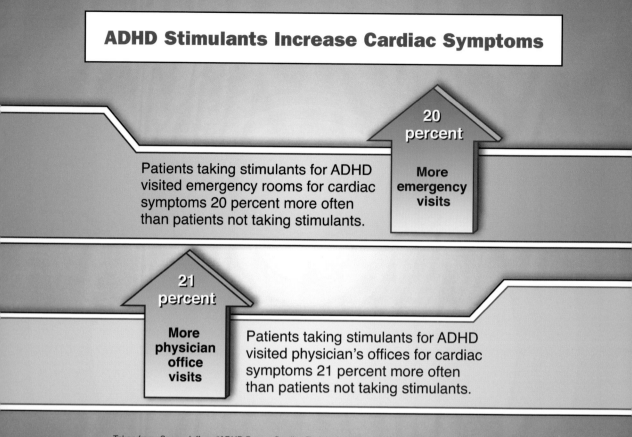

ADHD Stimulants Increase Cardiac Symptoms

Patients taking stimulants for ADHD visited emergency rooms for cardiac symptoms 20 percent more often than patients not taking stimulants.

20 percent

More emergency visits

21 percent

More physician office visits

Patients taking stimulants for ADHD visited physician's offices for cardiac symptoms 21 percent more often than patients not taking stimulants.

Taken from: Susan Jeffery, "ADHD Drugs: Cardiac Toxicity Low, but Emergency Room Visits Up," The Heart.org, December 18, 2007.

academic, occupational and interpersonal failure, sexual promiscuity and increased risk of cigarette smoking, criminality and motor vehicle accidents. Stimulant medications, such as methylphenidate [Ritalin] and amphetamines, have been used to effectively treat this disorder for more than 30 years in both the United States and abroad. Global use of ADHD medications rose threefold from 1993 through 2003, whereas global spending (U.S. $2.4 billion in 2003) rose ninefold. In the United States, use of these medications increased fourfold in the decade, beginning in the mid 1980's, but appears to have leveled off in the most recent decade. The scope of the problem is illustrated by estimates that currently in the United States these medications are prescribed for approximately 2.5 million pediatric patients annually.

Using ECGs to Prevent Sudden Cardiac Death in Children Taking Stimulants

Given the sympathomimetic[1] qualities of the stimulant medications, it is not surprising that minor changes in heart rate and blood pressure have been reported. However, when use of these medications was previously reviewed by the Council on Cardiovascular Disease in the Young in 1999, no specific cardiovascular monitoring was recommended; though, since that time, important issues have surfaced necessitating a second look at this problem. Awareness of ADHD in both the general pediatric population, as well as in children with underlying cardiac conditions, has continued to increase. There have been public concerns about the side effects and toxicities of medications in general but especially of stimulant medications in children. However, the major concerns have stemmed from reports of sudden cardiac death (SCD) in children taking these medications. Despite the low prevalence, the emotional effect of SCD in a child, on the family, and the community is disproportionately large (high-grief death) due in part to the youth, apparent good health, and lost potential. The recent recommendation for a "Black-Box Warning" (a type of warning that appears on the package insert for prescription drugs that may cause serious adverse effects) has added considerably to anxiety regarding the safety of these medications.

In [the April 22, 2008] issue of *Circulation*, [cardiologist Victoria] Vetter and associates provide a timely and comprehensive overview of ADHD in the general population and in children with heart disease, and they give a detailed account of the regulatory issues that have surfaced since 2005. The authors review etiology [cause], risk factors, and prevention of SCD in the young. As part of the assessment of efforts to prevent SCD in the pediatric

---

[1] *Sympathomimetic* refers to drugs that stimulate the nervous system, like adrenaline.

population, the authors provide informative updates of worldwide initiatives focusing on universal electrocardiogram (ECG) screening and the role of ECG and echocardiography in preparticipation screening of athletes. The report also provides a comprehensive update on pharmacotherapy of ADHD, including cardiovascular side effects. Based on this background, the authors develop guidelines, patterned after recommendations, to screen for SCD risk. . . . To increase the likelihood of identifying significant cardiac conditions known to be associated with SCD, the group recommends that all patients have an electrocardiogram prior to commencing stimulant medications.

Like motherhood and apple pie, prevention of SCD, especially in the young, is championed by most. Risk as-

A young man waits to take an electrocardiogram (ECG) of his heart. The American Heart Association recommends ECGs for children for whom stimulants have been prescribed for ADHD. (AP Images)

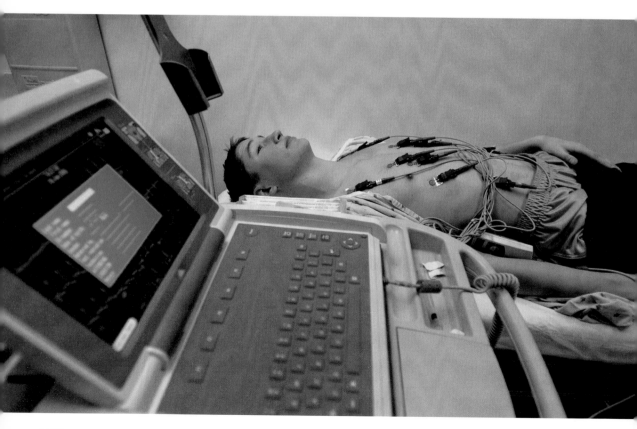

sessment is an important component of the preventive strategy. Reservations regarding risk assessment are usually related to expense and concerns about sensitivity (the extent to which at-risk individuals can be identified) and specificity (mislabeling normal individuals as affected). These latter concerns have certainly been true for the EGG and are the basis for [cardiologist Barry] Maron [and colleagues] to conclude that mass ECG screening of competitive athletes was not feasible. In regard to expense, Vetter [and associates] argue, "The use of selective ECG screening in this population is felt to be medically indicated and of reasonable cost."

> **FAST FACT**
>
> According to the American Heart Association, about thirty-six thousand children are born with a congenital heart defect each year.

The authors of this AHA Scientific Statement are to be congratulated for their thorough review of ADHD, the pharmacotherapy of ADHD medications, and stimulant medication associated SCD. Nonetheless, it remains unclear whether the risk for SCD is actually higher in patients receiving stimulant medications than it is in the general pediatric population. From a practical standpoint, the rarity of this problem means that it may be impossible to develop evidence-based guidelines for cardiovascular monitoring of children and adolescents receiving stimulant drugs. The Agency for Healthcare Research and Quality (AHRQ) and the FDA [Food and Drug Administration], are funding a retrospective study being coordinated by Vanderbilt University to perform a review of data of 500,000 children and adults to determine whether medications used to treat ADHD increase cardiac-risk factors. More data defining cardiac risk may help to frame the scope of the problem.

The guidelines proposed in the paper by Vetter and colleagues serve a useful purpose to bring an important concern to the forefront. Certainly, in pediatric patients known to have heart disease, a comprehensive and thoughtful diagnostic and surveillance strategy is mandatory. However, since most stimulant medications are prescribed by general and subspecialty pediatricians, psychiatrists, and family practitioners, for the proposed guidelines to become a standard of care, a consensus involving the providers who prescribe these medications and their respective professional organizations should be sought.

Children Do Not Need to Undergo Heart Screening Before Taking Stimulants to Treat ADHD

Lawrence Diller

In the following viewpoint Lawrence Diller contends that the American Heart Association (AHA) is overreacting when it recommends that children should have electrocardiograms before taking stimulants to treat attention deficit hyperactivity disorder (ADHD). He asserts that the chances of a child dying suddenly from heart problems associated with Ritalin, Adderall, or other stimulants prescribed to treat ADHD are extremely small. He believes the AHA was being alarmist when it made its recommendations. Lawrence Diller is a behavioral pediatrician, professor, and the author of the book *The Last Normal Child*.

O n April 21st [2008] the American Heart Association (AHA) shocked families and professionals alike when it recommended that all kids that take or may take Ritalin should have an electrocardiogram (ECG). Stimulant drugs like Ritalin, Concerta and Adderall have been used in children for ADHD for

SOURCE: Lawrence Diller, "ECG's, ADHD, Ritalin . . . Oh My!" www.docdiller.com, 2008. Reproduced by permission.

70 years. Why this recommendation now—and should you get one for your child if he/she takes one of these drugs?

Trying to Make Sense of the AHA Recommendations

I read and reread the article in *Circulation* (the official journal of the AHA) four times trying to make sense of the main points and recommendations. I've spoken to two high up academic child psychiatrists. I am awaiting a call back from my contact pediatric cardiologist. We've consulted before on a boy with severe ADHD whom I've treated with Concerta who also has had surgical repair of his heart that was missing his left ventricle when he was born.

The AHA evaluation and recommendations were prompted by reports two years ago [2006] of the sudden deaths of 18 children while taking a prescription stimulant drug over a five year period (1999 to 2004). Only seven of these children were found not to have structural heart problems. Their deaths were felt to be caused by severe irregular heart beats associated with their basic cardiac condition and exacerbated by taking the medication.

For six months the Canadian equivalent of the FDA [U.S. Food and Drug Administration] banned Adderall (felt to be the drug of most concern) for children in Canada. However, after considering all the numbers (how many children take the drug) and the relative risk, the ban was rescinded. Now come the AHA recommendations that include obtaining an ECG for any child (even those without any cardiac symptom or family history) being considered for a prescription stimulant. The AHA recommends that all children currently on stimulants

> **FAST FACT**
>
> It is estimated that about 1 in every 1,000 adults aged thirty-five or older and 0.5 to 1 in every 100,000 children suffers from sudden cardiac death each year, according to the American Heart Association.

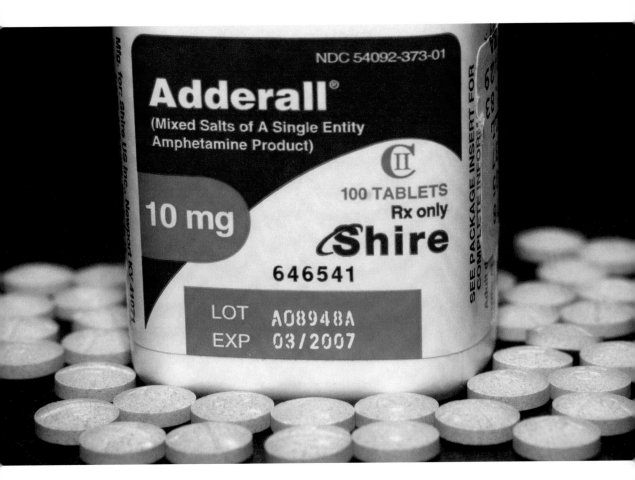

also get an ECG. Also if the first ECG was obtained before the age of twelve a second ECG should be performed when the child is a teenager.

I commented on this problem of sudden death two years ago. Most of you [who are] aware of my writing and stance know that I've been prescribing stimulant medication to children for thirty years even as I feel we over prescribe and don't sufficiently pursue effective non-drug interventions for problems of children's behavior and performance (at school). I've never felt that stimulants were dangerous and I believe they are effective in the short term. My calls for caution were based more [on] ethical than medical reasons.

The viewpoint's author argues against the American Heart Association's recommendation that children with ADHD be given an ECG prior to being prescribed drugs such as Adderall. (JB Reed/Bloomberg News/ Landov)

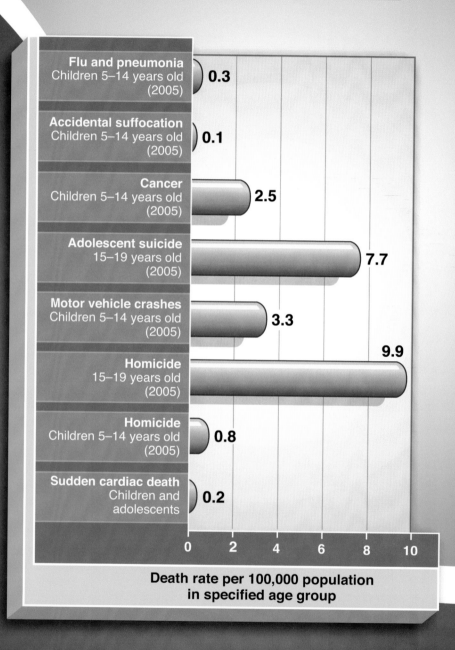

Causes of Death in Children and Adolescents, 2005

Flu and pneumonia
Children 5–14 years old
(2005)
0.3

Accidental suffocation
Children 5–14 years old
(2005)
0.1

Cancer
Children 5–14 years old
(2005)
2.5

Adolescent suicide
15–19 years old
(2005)
7.7

Motor vehicle crashes
Children 5–14 years old
(2005)
3.3

Homicide
15–19 years old
(2005)
9.9

Homicide
Children 5–14 years old
(2005)
0.8

Sudden cardiac death
Children and
adolescents
0.2

0   2   4   6   8   10

Death rate per 100,000 population in specified age group

Taken from: Department of Health and Human Services, "Child Health USA 2007," 2005 data./American Academy of Pediatrics, "Policy Statement: Cardiovascular Monitoring and Stimulant Drugs for Attention Deficit Hyperactivity Disorder," May 28, 2008.

Infinitesimal Risk

Two years ago I tried to figure the risk for a child without heart disease of dying suddenly while taking a stimulant. I used seven as the numerator—the number of kids who died without heart disease present—and four million as the denominator—my estimate of the number of kids under the age of eighteen taking stimulant drugs in America in 2006. I came up with a number with five zeroes after the decimal point (.00000175) or 0.000175 per cent, approximately two ten thousandths of a per cent chance of dying suddenly if the child is taking a stimulant drug. This represents what I call an "existential" level of risk.

I am not certain of my numbers but suggested the likelihood of getting killed on the local freeway on a Saturday night by a drunk driver was probably higher—and still we take freeways because it gets us from one place to another faster. I'm not sure what the accident rate on surface roads is but it's all meaningless in terms of real risk—much like debating how many angels [can] dance on the head of a pin.

Even taking eighteen as the numerator and lowering the denominator to 2.5 million (the CDC [U.S. Centers for Disease Control and Prevention] estimate of the number of children taking stimulants) one gets about four times the risk—now seven ten thousandths per cent—but still infinitesimal. So why did the AHA make their recommendation?

Cynical Reasons

I could answer cynically and say this was a real CYA [cover your ass] move so that the AHA and pediatric cardiologists could tell child psychiatrists, pediatricians and family physicians, "See we gave you our warning," should the public mood ever change over the propriety of the widespread use of stimulant drugs in children. But the AHA recommendation brings up an ethical dilemma for parents (and doctors) who want to feel that they took every possible precaution in the unlikely event (and we're talking on the level of lightning strikes or lotto winners) a catastrophe occurred.

The AHA acknowledges that an abnormal ECG alone does not represent a complete contraindication towards using a stimulant drug for a child. Rather AHA experts suggest the family and pediatric cardiologist discuss the relative risks. I suppose in a truly borderline decision it might psychologically (because scientifically, the risk is so, so low) have a family lean towards not using the medication for the child. As someone who feels the medication is generally over prescribed I suppose I should be pleased with this result but I'm not if the basis is a hysteria over existential risk.

Parents Should Decide

I am planning to let parents decide for themselves. I will give them my opinion that I am willing to assume the theoretical added risk in not knowing whether or not a child has asymptomatic cardiac disease. However, if the family wants to obtain an ECG for their child I will support it. I suspect some of the more anxious parents will opt to get the ECG for their kid. Has anyone in this imbroglio figured in the slightly higher rates of suicidality when one prescribes an SSRI [selective serotonin reuptake inhibitor] to an anxious child? Confronting hypocrisy and propaganda has routinely been my motive for speaking out and writing. Overreaction and hysteria even in well thought out scenarios require my challenging the "authorities" again.

CHAPTER 3

Personal Experiences with ADHD

My Life Changed for the Better After My ADHD Diagnosis and Treatment

Ann Barkin, as told to Sandy Fertman Ryan

In the following viewpoint Ann Barkin provides a young girl's perspective of living with attention deficit hyperactivity disorder (ADHD). Barkin says she used to feel different from other kids. Her school life and her social life were complicated and unpleasant. She could not keep up with her homework, and she was bullied and teased at school. Things changed, however, after she was diagnosed with ADHD and began taking medication. Barkin explains that she does not feel so different from other kids anymore. Ann Barkin is a sixteen-year-old high school student. She told her story to writer Sandy Fertman Ryan for the magazine *Girl's Life*.

Photo on previous page. Children suffering from ADHD often are bullied and teased in school by fellow students. (© Bubbles Photolibrary/ Alamy)

When I was little, I thought I was just like any other kid. But by fourth grade, I was sure there was something different about me. I couldn't keep up in school, and I found it impossible—no matter how hard I tried—to pay attention in class. I thought I wasn't as smart as other kids.

SOURCE: Ann Barkin and Sandy Fertman Ryan, "Out of Focus," *Girls' Life*, vol. 13, August/September 2006, pp. 66–68. Reproduced by permission.

As I got older, my problems got worse. I would get so disorganized that I'd lose my school work before handing it in. My teachers constantly told my parents, "We don't doubt Ann's doing the homework. She's smart and really understands the topic. But it's just not getting to the teacher and we don't know why." I had no clue something called Attention-Deficit/Hyperactive Disorder (ADHD) even existed.

From Bad to Much Worse

By eighth grade, things were out of control. Although I was in honors math, I had such a hard time focusing and getting assignments in that I had to quit. I felt like a failure. I pretty much daydreamed through class because it was impossible for me to sit still. As my workload increased, my problems escalated. I think everyone thought I was this spaced-out, stupid weirdo.

My school life and social life were a mess. I was never invited to parties, and I gained a ton of weight with all the stress. I became the girl who was bullied by a gang of about 20 kids. Luckily, I had the best group of friends a girl could ask for. They were always there for me.

Even so, I often came home from school crying. The mean kids made every day a nightmare, calling me names like "Fatty" or "Stupid." One of the worst days was when we were playing soccer outside during gym and this boy kept hitting me with the ball—and it really stung. I'd yell, "Stop it!" But he kept doing it, and all the kids just laughed at me. I was so humiliated. I tried to act like it didn't bother me but, when I got to my next class and saw two of my friends, I broke down.

Those kids did tons of other horrible things to me that year. Guys came up to me in study hall and said, "Hey, Ann, wanna go out with me?" with all of their friends watching. It was very obvious that they weren't really asking me out, and it was embarrassing. No matter how I responded, they'd all laugh. My mom said, "They're just jerks!" But I figured she had to say that since she's my mom.

Even with the support of my parents and friends, I didn't see any way out. I figured I was and always would be this stupid, fat, lazy, unpopular kid.

Desperate for Answers

By then, my self-esteem was pretty much non-existent. But I never sat around wishing I could be like the popular kids—I just wanted to be the kid who wasn't picked on. I worked incredibly hard to get good grades, but I failed Spanish and basically had all C's and some D's. My par-

Children with ADHD have trouble concentrating in school, but drugs like Concerta may improve their concentration and academic achievement. (© David Young-Wolff/Alamy)

ents were concerned so, in desperation, my mom discussed the problem with my guidance counselor. She said my inattentiveness and lack of focus were "just a phase." Right! Like, my whole life was a phase. Meanwhile, I scored in the top percentiles on standardized tests, but my report-card marks were terrible.

The last straw was in ninth grade. I'd always imagined things would be better in high school, but my grades were still terrible. My parents took me to a professional to gauge my study habits. After a few days of testing, the man said I had very clear signs of ADHD. I was like, "What's that?"

"You have trouble concentrating and are hyperactive because of a chemical imbalance or an irregularity in the way your brain works," he explained. He also added that having ADHD didn't mean I was stupid—it just meant I couldn't focus. Hearing that was such a relief.

Although there's no cure for ADHD, I was prescribed Concerta for my symptoms. My mom felt bad for not taking me to get help sooner, but I never blamed my parents—they've been completely supportive, even when they had no clue what was wrong with me.

FAST FACT

In their first two to five years of driving, youth with ADHD have nearly four times as many automobile accidents; are more likely to cause bodily injury in accidents; and have three times as many citations for speeding as young drivers without ADHD, according to psychologist Russell Barkley in *Taking Charge of ADHD.*

Everything Changed with Medication

As weird as it sounds, after learning I had ADHD, my first thought was, "I can get through this myself." I was in denial because I didn't want to admit anything was wrong with me. Being on medication made me feel like a freak.

Since I was so firm about not taking Concerta, my parents made a deal with me that I wouldn't have to take it if I worked extra hard for the next two weeks to show them I didn't need it. But after two weeks, there was no change, so my parents said, "At least try the Concerta. If you don't like it, you can always stop." I started taking it with a completely negative attitude, almost willing it not to work. But right away, everything changed. I immediately got better grades, and my homework was getting in on time. By the end of the year, I had all A's and B's. I went from flunking Spanish to winning the Spanish Award.

I felt so good that I lost 20 pounds in a year and have since lost 13 more. I joined swim team and drama club, and my social life is great. At first, I didn't tell anyone except my best friend about my ADHD. But the more I talked to people about it, the more I realized having ADHD is no big deal.

For the first time, I don't feel so different from everyone. I'm more active, open and confident. I'm no longer the one everyone picks on—and I love that I still have problems with organizational skills, but I have a tutor who helps.

Positive Aspects of ADHD

Looking back, I feel great knowing all the bad stuff that happened to me wasn't my fault—I wasn't stupid after all! I'm sure if I'd known I had ADHD, things would have been different then.

Even though I hated finding out I have ADHD, I've learned there actually are a lot of positive things about having it. People with ADHD are creative, energetic and passionate. And for me, that makes me really good at writing, drama and brainstorming ideas.

Living with the Tics That Accompany My ADHD

Blake E.S. Taylor

In the following viewpoint excerpted from his memoir, *ADHD & Me*, Blake E.S. Taylor provides a glimpse into a day of living with attention deficit hyperactivity disorder (ADHD). Taylor describes one day in sixth grade when he was giving a speech and had an episode of tics. According to the author, tics are a common coexisting condition with ADHD. Taylor wrote *ADHD & Me* during his last two years of high school. After high school he began attending the University of California.

Sixth grade. History class. Thirty minutes until lunch. I'm beginning my presentation about the Roman conquest of Carthage. About two minutes into the presentation, I feel a tic coming. I attempt to repress it, but my effort is useless. I jerk my neck backward and then forward. The whole class stares at me. I rub the back of

SOURCE: Blake E.S. Taylor, *ADHD & Me: What I Learned from Lighting Fires at the Dinner Table*. Oakland: New Harbinger Publications, Inc., 2008. Copyright © 2007 by Blake Taylor. Reproduced by permission.

my neck to pretend that I am just relieving neck pain, and my attempt to cover up the tic works; the students in my class look away, having dismissed the possibility that there is really something wrong with me, that the tic is a sign of some mental condition.

However, a minute later, I'm on the verge of another tic. I'm talking faster about the Carthaginian general Hannibal and the elephants he used in battle. The tic is coming. Now, I'm talking about the Roman catapult and how the Romans could build such an engineering marvel in the field of battle. The tic happens, and the class stares at me a second time, but they stare more thoroughly this time, as if thinking, "We did see something very odd," and now they watch to see if it will happen again. I rub the back of my neck again, and I "cover" the tic. But a minute later, I have another tic. I rub the back of my neck again, but I'm not convincing anyone this time.

"Now They Will Think of Me as Odd"

My social studies teacher, Ms. Lea Wedge Morrison, looks at me with a concerned expression, and when I make eye contact with her, she interrupts my presentation and says, "Blake, are you okay?" She is a beautiful blonde with sparkling eyes who makes history exciting for us.

I answer, "Oh, yes, my neck is just bothering me."

I look at my classmates, who are now scrutinizing my every movement. I'm finished with my presentation. And they will never regard me the same way again.

My family and I have just moved in the middle of sixth grade from a little town in Weston, Connecticut, to a suburb of San Francisco. I have wanted so much to make a good impression on my new classmates. I wanted them to like my presentation and, therefore, to like me. Now, they will think of me as odd—and as one of the ones to be dismissed. I feel defeated—just like Hannibal.

The viewpoint's author, Blake Taylor, relates his life experiences as an ADHD sufferer in his book *ADHD & Me*. **(Kristopher Skinner/ MCT/Landov)**

Coexisting Conditions

The incident in sixth grade was just one of many situations I've lived through as I have struggled over and over again with a tic condition, which often can accompany ADHD. Some young people with ADHD also have tics. In fact, scientists have found that two-thirds of children with ADHD have at least one other coexisting condition. Simple tics and Tourette's syndrome seem to commonly occur with ADHD.

Simple tics are sudden, repetitive, involuntary movements or sounds. They can include such behaviors as eye blinking, mouth opening, sniffing, throat clearing, or head movements. Usually, simple tics are temporary; they come and go and last for less than a year. Suddenly they disappear, but they can change and reappear again at a later time.

Tourette's syndrome is a little different. It is a condition that includes vocal tics along with motor tics; both vocal and motor tics have to last for more than one year for the condition to be diagnosed as Tourette's [according to the National Resource Center on ADHD]. Vocal tics include throat clearing, coughing, barking, or repeating words or phrases; they may also include screaming and saying some bad words. Motor tics can range from simple movements like eye blinking, lip licking, grimacing, or mouth opening, to more complex movements, like head jerking or shoulder shrugging. Tourette's syndrome is usually mild, and it is often accompanied by other conditions—ADHD being the most likely. Sixty percent of children with Tourette's also have ADHD. The main difference between simple tics and Tourette's is that with simple tics, the tics come and go. With Tourette's, tics persist; they don't go away.

FAST FACT

In 2006 ADHD prompted about 7 million visits to doctors' offices, emergency rooms, or outpatient clinics, according to the National Center for Health Statistics.

Neutralizing Tics

My doctors believe that I have a simple tic disorder that is chronic, meaning that a tic will appear at certain times, especially when I am nervous, and then disappear. The tic changes and comes back, only to disappear again. As far as I know, my tics first appeared when I was very young. Over time, they became stronger and stronger, and to counteract them, my doctor gave me clonidine, a blood pressure medicine, to take along with the stimulant medications I was taking for ADHD. The clonidine worked for a while, but my doctor had to keep increasing the dosage to help neutralize the tics. When a new medication for ADHD—Strattera—was introduced, my doctor switched me to that, and the tics lessened considerably and almost disappeared. I say "almost," because tics have reappeared during stressful times, whether it was moving, changing schools, meeting new people, taking final exams, or interviewing for high schools. Tics also can occur when you are tired.

Many Kinds of Tics

I, myself, have had several kinds of tics—and I must admit that some of them were quite bizarre. When I was in third grade, I had a motion tic in which I had to twirl in a circle. This twirling created an imaginary spiral of bricks around me, and every time I twirled, another layer of bricks was added. I twirled in one direction, but then I was obligated to twirl in the other direction in order to feel balanced. If I did not complete the cycle four times, my mind did not seem satisfied. Eventually, after four cycles, I found I would become dizzy and would be forced to stop.

In fifth grade, I had a rather unusual tic—banging my chest and making a noise while I did it, almost like Tarzan. But I wasn't trying to be like Tarzan. I did it because I felt a shaking in my lung when this tic occurred. After completing the cycle of the tic, I would feel better and could continue with whatever I was doing at the time.

In seventh grade, I had a vocal tic in which I continued to repeat "101." This is the highway number of the Bayshore Freeway leading to San Francisco. Something about the rhythm of the words captured me, and the tic started. There was comfort in repeating and making the numbers resonate: "1 . . . 0 . . . 1 (Hey!) 1 . . . 0 . . . 1."

Another, more recent tic occurred in ninth grade. This tic was more sedate and more common looking—blinking. I would blink my eyes repeatedly to feel the pressure of my eyelid against my eye until the tic was satisfied.

The basic fact about tics is that I am actually reluctant to have them. Yet even though these tics persist, my mind never seems completely satisfied. When one tic ends, there may be nothing for a while. And then suddenly, another one begins. I have minimal control over which tic will come next, and it usually is a total surprise.

Unconscious Yet Conscious

Tics are not conscious, yet they are not totally unconscious. They are, instead, something in between.

My mother often pleads with me to stop the tics. "Blake, can you control this?" she asks. "Blake, can you stop this? Please don't do this. People are looking at you. People will wonder why you are doing that."

And she doesn't like the answer I give her. I say, "I can —and I can't—control the tics."

"What do you mean, you can and you can't? Either you can or you can't." She becomes exasperated.

I cannot tell you how many hundreds of times we've had this same discussion. The reason is that tics do not occur entirely by themselves. I consciously make the effort to move whichever muscle is needed to execute the tic. However, this conscious effort is driven by an unconscious inclination, almost a warning or a signal, that a tic is on the way. I think about how I will feel if I were to turn in a circle, or repeat certain words, and then, unable to resist, I allow the tic to happen.

My Son's Story

Laurie Hagberg

In the following viewpoint teacher Laurie Hagberg describes the struggles she has had with her son, who has attention deficit hyperactivity disorder (ADHD), and how these struggles have made her a better teacher. Hagberg says she used to be skeptical of parents who came to her asking for understanding about their ADHD children. However, after the birth of her son, Jonathan, she learned how real ADHD is and the difficulties these kids face in school. She hopes that by telling Jonathan's story she will help other teachers better understand the children with ADHD in their own classrooms. Since 1998, Hagberg has maintained a Web site aimed at informing parents and teachers about children with ADHD and other special-needs.

I n 1991, when my son was born, I considered myself a fairly competent teacher. True, I was strict, but not unreasonable. Yes, I expected certain classroom behaviors, but not the impossible. I've since realized that there was much then that I didn't know about my students—or about my son.

SOURCE: Laurie Hagberg, "My Son's Story and How This Site Began . . . ," http://adhd.kids.tripod.com, 2008. Reproduced by permission.

An Unhappy Child

When my son was a baby, he cried all of the time—not the scrunch-up-the-knees colic cry—but a full breath-stopping wail that could last up to an hour and a half! This crying was inconsolable and seemed to be triggered by an event or outing. He would be as happy as can be, for instance, during a trip to the mall; upon arrival home, however, he screamed as if he were the most miserable little baby alive. I can remember times when I couldn't hold him close enough, couldn't calm his spirit, couldn't sit and listen to him any longer, crying myself and asking God why He gave this little boy life if he was going to be so unhappy.

Behavioral problems associated with children with ADHD can start well before preschool, leading to aggressive behavior against peers when a youngster enters school. (© Bubbles Photolibrary/Alamy)

By his second year of preschool, my husband and I knew our son was not like other kids—he seemed to have special needs—needs we weren't sure how to meet. For instance, we realized that our son couldn't follow directions —not *wouldn't*—*couldn't*. We learned to take him by the shoulders, look into his eyes, and say, "Focus." We asked his preschool teachers to do the same—it helped him to listen to us and "focus" on what we were saying—something we now know his brain does not allow him to do easily.

Always "in Trouble"

As the preschool years came to an end, our son experienced several drastic behavioral changes—he was "in trouble" a lot. He lashed out aggressively toward other kids, he would get a vacant look in his eyes during times his behavior was most out of control, and at times, he would become so enraged with something "gone wrong" that I would literally have to sit on the floor with him, my arms and legs "wrapped" tightly around him to get him to calm down. Kindergarten loomed ahead, and we prayed that the newness of learning would grab our son's mind and reduce the frequency of the preschool behaviors that were possibly caused by mental boredom.

ADHD Diagnosis

We were blessed with a wonderful teacher that first year who had a gift for loving difficult children—children like our son! She willingly answered his questions, she willingly met with us as we faced his challenging behavior in class, and she patiently and prayerfully worked with him as he went through the ADHD diagnosis process. ADHD diagnosis entailed several visits to a specialist recommended by our school's high school guidance counselor. We and our son's teacher completed evaluation forms about what we had observed, and the doctor prescribed Zoloft to raise the seratonin levels and Adderall to establish a balanced adrenaline level. This was not a quick and easy process. We all experienced "the weeks from hell" when the dosage wasn't quite right. Eventually, however, by the end of the kindergarten year, our son's diagnosis and prescriptions were established. During that time, we also learned that any foods or drinks with red dye increase his out-of-control behaviors, while a bit of coffee helps calm our son. We have had to research and reassess many environmental factors related to ADHD. In addition, as our son has grown, the medications have had to be adjusted—there is no "one-time" "this-is-all-you-need" fix for ADHD.

Traumatic School Years

Jonathan's school years, since kindergarten, have been traumatic due to his own behaviors and the misunderstandings that come when a teacher or administrator does not understand ADHD beyond the "attention problems." His first grade teacher never even tried to understand—for you who are parents, do not give up advocating for your child even if a teacher is "older and, supposedly, wiser"— for you who are teachers, do not ignore any information offered to you to help you understand your students (and their parents) better. By the spring of his second grade year, we knew we had to find a different school for Jonathan. The principal of his school did not have the background knowledge or concern to deal with Jonathan—in fact, one evening he called my husband and me at home to ask that we keep Jonathan home the next day because Jonathan's teacher (the principal's wife) had requested it. I asked if Jonathan was being suspended for some behavior problem, and the principal responded that no, it wasn't that—it was just that his wife felt she and the class needed a break from Jonathan.

Jonathan did not go back to that classroom. He stayed with my sister for a week while my husband and I prayed and looked for another school to put him in for the rest of the year. The Lord led us to a school called Light and

Life, in our neighborhood, which though smaller, had teachers and a principal who were educated in how to work with kids like Jonathan. He finished up third grade at that school. The first three years of elementary school took their toll on Jonathan and our family. We found ourselves emotionally drained and decided to move closer to family for support. The following year was another experience of educating a teacher, but we did have the support of an educated principal at Fresno Christian elementary who met with us and Jonathan's teacher frequently to develop preventive and positive strategies to help Jonathan succeed. The year was difficult, but he did make it through. The following year he was homeschooled by a relative who gave very little work—he essentially played outside for most of his fifth grade year (the year was also unusual in that due to unexpected circumstances, we were living in the living room of my in-laws for a year!). In sixth grade, after yet another family move, Jonathan struggled to get back into the routine and discipline of yet another school, but that proved more than he or the school could handle. The following year he entered seventh grade, in a public school. Two years later, we proudly watched as he walked across the stage, graduating from eighth grade—despite missing the last week of classes due to his inability to handle major changes/endings. When Jonathan applied to the school he currently attends, he was denied admittance due to his past. After many people's prayers and our formal appeals, minds and hearts were opened and Jonathan was admitted. The first week of school, he met another student who, like Jonathan, plays online games; the second week of school, he spent the night at this new friend's house. I cry as I recall his excitement—due to moving and social issues,

> **FAST FACT**
>
> According to the National Center for Health Statistics, ADHD limits the normal activities of eighteen to twenty-two out of every one thousand U.S. children between the ages of five and seventeen.

Jonathan had never had a friend before, let alone one who invited him over. Now, as a junior, Jonathan not only has that first friend, but many others—and he manages to earn grades of Cs and Bs (not without struggle, but still he does it)! Jonathan is a survivor, he is improving, and we try to stay patient with him as he's now at the age of wanting more independence and less parental-interference.

I imagine that each new school year will bring anxiety and fear of what the year ahead will hold for Jonathan and us. We are thankful for this school, Oaks Christian—one which has caring, informed administrators and staff. So we pray together, Jonathan once again packs his backpack, and we remind ourselves that the Lord has brought us this far, He will see His work through to completion.

The Teacher Learns

I've come to realize that the learning is not over for me as a parent or as a teacher. My husband and I know now that a blissful home-life each day after school is probably an illusion. We accept this, and understanding why our son behaves as he does, we try to help him develop the strengths he does have. And perhaps, just as important, I have an understanding of why some of my students behave as they do. Since my son started school, I've had to step back and look at some of my classroom practices and realize that I've hurt kids in the past because I did expect the impossible of them. I decided that I wanted to share my experiences with other teachers—teachers who, like me, may be skeptical of the various disorders and the requests of parents. . . .

You see, in 1991, I didn't believe in ADHD. I thought it was an excuse parents used when they weren't willing to hold their child accountable. I assumed the student was lazy. I responded to the student's behaviors accordingly, with harsh judgment and actions. Oh, I look back now and ache for those kids—kids whom I didn't understand. Was I unfair? Possibly. Was I willfully unfair? No. Was I ignorant? Yes.

Painful Lessons

A few years ago, a parent of a former student of mine reminded me of the teacher I used to be. She recalled that in the spring before I was to have her son in class, she wanted to talk to me about his ADD [attention deficit disorder] and problems he would have in class. Tears filled her eyes as she remembered my response—one I've now tried to block from memory—one she did not deserve. She is now a good friend of mine and we've shared tears and smiles about both of our sons (her son graduated from high school and is now successfully employed!). I needed to have a son with special needs to become the teacher my students needed me to be. I didn't know that, when my son was born—I am absolutely certain of it, though, now. Lessons learned painfully—to prevent hurting those in my care. It is my prayer that as teachers learn more about their students as individuals, more individuals will look back and say, "Thank you for understanding me."

GLOSSARY

Adderall A brand-name stimulant drug that contains a combination of mixed amphetamine salts. It is used to improve attention span and decrease impulsivity (*see also* **amphetamine**).

amphetamine A central nervous system stimulant that acts by increasing levels of norepinephrine, serotonin, and dopamine in the brain.

anxiety A feeling of apprehension and fear characterized by physical symptoms such as palpitations, sweating, and feelings of stress.

atomoxetine A nonstimulant drug approved for the treatment of ADHD. Atomoxetine is classified as a norepinephrine (noradrenaline) reuptake inhibitor (*see also* **Strattera**).

attention The act or state of focusing on a selected stimulus, sustaining that focus, and shifting it at will.

attention deficit disorder (ADD) An older term frequently used to describe individuals who have attention deficit hyperactivity disorder without the hyperactive and impulsive behaviors. This term has generally been replaced with the term *ADHD*—inattentive type.

attention deficit hyperactivity disorder (ADHD) A family of related chronic neurobiological disorders that interfere with an individual's capacity to regulate activity level (hyperactivity), inhibit behavior (impulsivity), and attend to tasks (inattention) in developmentally appropriate ways.

attention deficit hyperactivity disorder— hyperactive impulsive type One of two categories of ADHD recognized by the *Diagnostic and Statistical Manual of Mental Disorders, 4th edition* (*DSM-IV*). This category is used to describe people with ADHD who exhibit primarily hyperactive and impulsive behaviors.

attention deficit hyperactivity disorder— inattentive type	One of two categories of ADHD recognized by the *DSM-IV*. This category is used to describe people with ADHD who exhibit primarily inattentive behaviors; previously called attention deficit disorder.
behavior therapy	A treatment program that involves substituting desirable behavior responses for undesirable ones.
bipolar disorder	A depressive disorder in which a person alternates between episodes of major depression and mania.
cerebral cortex	The outer portion of the brain, which plays a key role in memory, attention, perceptual awareness, thought, language, and consciousness.
clinical psychologist	A psychologist who teaches about, researches, or treats persons with any of the common mental health disorders. Clinical psychologists generally use psychotherapy, not medications, to treat mental health disorders.
cognitive	Pertaining to cognition, the process of knowing and, more precisely, the process of being aware, knowing, thinking, learning, and judging.
comorbidity	The coexistence of two or more disease processes.
conduct disorder	A behavioral and emotional disorder of childhood and adolescence. Children with conduct disorder act inappropriately, infringe on the rights of others, and violate the behavioral expectations of others.
cultural construct	An anthropological term that indicates something that is culturally defined.
depression	A mood disorder characterized by a range of symptoms that may include feeling depressed most of the time, loss of pleasure, feelings of worthlessness, suicidal thoughts, as well as physical states that may affect eating and sleeping and other activities.

developmental disability	A term used to describe lifelong disabilities attributable to mental and/or physical impairments, manifested prior to age twenty-two.
developmental disorder	Disorders that occur at some stage in a child's development, often retarding development. These may include psychological or physical disorders.
Diagnostic and Statistical Manual of Mental Disorders, 4th Edition (DSM-IV)	A book published by the American Psychiatric Association that gives general descriptions and characteristic symptoms of mental illnesses. Physicians and other mental health professionals use the *DSM-IV* to confirm diagnoses for mental illnesses.
dopamine	A neurotransmitter known to have multiple functions depending on where it acts. Dopamine is thought to regulate emotional responses and to play a role in schizophrenia and cocaine abuse.
DRD4 7R	A gene associated with ADHD that codes for a protein that recognizes dopamine.
electrocardiogram (ECG)	A test that measures and records the electrical activity of the heart.
electroencephalography (EEG)	A test that measures and records the electrical activity of the brain.
hyperactive child syndrome	The term used by Stella Chase in 1960 to describe for the first time a condition of hyperactivity that was not due to brain damage.
hyperactivity	A higher-than-normal level of activity.
hyperkinetic reaction of childhood	The term used in the *Diagnostic and Statistical Manual of Mental Disorders, 2nd edition (DSM-II)* in the 1960s to describe a condition characterized by a short attention span, hyperactivity, and restlessness; i.e., what we generally know today as ADHD—hyperactive impulsive type.

impulsivity	Inclined to act on impulse rather than thought. People who are overly impulsive seem unable to curb their immediate reactions or to think before they act.
learning disabilities	A group of disorders that affect a broad range of academic and functional skills, including the ability to speak, listen, read, write, spell, reason, and organize information.
magnetic resonance imaging (MRI)	A radiology technique that produces imges of interior body structures using magnetism, radio waves, and a computer.
methylphenidate	A central nervous system stimulant widely prescribed to treat ADHD (*see also* **Ritalin**).
minimal brain damage	A term introduced in the 1940s to describe ADHD-like symptoms that are thought to be caused by brain damage.
minimal brain dysfunction	One of various terms used in the 1950s and 1960s to describe mental deficiencies indicated by "hyperactive" behavior. Minimal brain dysfunction was formally defined in 1966 by Samuel Clements as a combination of average or above-average intelligence with certain mild to severe learning or behavioral disabilities characterizing deviant functioning of the central nervous system.
Multimodal Treatment Study of Children with ADHD (MTA)	The largest single study of the effectiveness of ADHD treatments. The MTA, which was sponsored by the National Institute of Mental Health, included six hundred elementary-school children at six different university medical centers.
neurons (nerve cells)	Specialized cells that carry "messages" through an electrochemical process that uses electrical signals and chemical substances called neurotransmitters.
neurotransmitters	Chemical substances that transmit information between neurons. Neurotransmitters are released by neurons into the extracellular space at synapses. There are several different neurotransmitters, including acetylcholine, dopamine, gamma aminobutyric acid (GABA), norepinephrine, and serotonin.

norepinephrine	Also called noradrenaline, it is a monoamine neurotransmitter produced both in the brain and in the peripheral nervous system. It seems to be involved in arousal, reward, regulation of sleep and mood, and the regulation of blood pressure.
obsessive compulsive disorder (OCD)	A chronic anxiety disorder most commonly characterized by obsessive, distressing, intrusive thoughts and related compulsions.
positron-emission tomography (PET)	A nuclear medicine imaging technique that measures gamma rays and reveals functional processes of the brain or other organs.
psychiatrist	A medical doctor who specializes in treating mental diseases. A psychiatrist evaluates a person's mental health along with his or her physical health and can prescribe medications.
psychologist	Someone who obtains a degree in psychology, which is the study of the "science of behavior."
psychotherapy	An interaction between a professional, typically a clinical psychologist, and a client that leads to changes—from a less adaptive state to a more adaptive state—in the client's thoughts, feelings, and behaviors.
Ritalin	A brand-name drug and one of the most common treatments for ADHD (*see also* **methylphenidate**).
Robins and Guze criteria	A set of criteria, developed in 1970, that helps doctors decide what constitutes a real and distinct psychiatric diagnosis.
serotonin	A monoamine neurotransmitter that regulates many functions, including mood, appetite, and sensory perception.
stimulants	A class of drugs that elevates mood, increases feelings of well-being, and increases energy and alertness.
Strattera	A brand-name drug that was the first nonstimulant treatment approved for ADHD (*see also* **atomoxetine**).

sudden cardiac death (SCD)	The sudden, abrupt loss of heart function in a person who may or may not have diagnosed heart disease. The time and mode of death are unexpected. It occurs instantly or shortly after symptoms appear.
tic	A repetitive movement that is difficult, if not impossible, to control. Tics can affect any group of muscles. The most common are facial tics, such as eye blinking, nose twitching, or grimacing. Tics that affect the muscles used to produce speech are known as vocal tics and can range from grunts or whistles to the repetition of complete words or phrases. Complex motor tics involve multiple, sequenced movements and can include behaviors such as twirling in place, tapping a certain number of times, or stooping to touch the ground. Tics are believed to arise in differences in or damage to the basal ganglia, a structure deep within the brain that controls automatic movements and that also affects impulsivity.
Tourette's syndrome	An inherited neuropsychiatric disorder with onset in childhood, characterized by the presence of multiple physical (motor) tics and at least one vocal tic.

CHRONOLOGY

B.C.   493   Hippocrates describes patients who have "quickened responses to sensory experience, but also less tenaciousness because the soul moves on quickly to the next impression."

A.D.   1845   Heinrich Hoffmann, a German physician and poet, writes a poem about a little boy named "Fidgety Phil," who could be interpreted as having ADHD.

1902   English pediatrician George Still describes a condition like ADHD; he calls it "morbid defect of moral control." Dr. Still's description is generally regarded as the first clinical description of ADHD.

1917–1918   A worldwide epidemic of encephalitis lethargica leaves many children and adults with behavioral and cognitive problems, including impulsivity, impaired attention, and other symptoms that correspond to ADHD. These children and adults are said to have post-encephalitic behavior disorders. This contributes to the notion that ADHD-like symptoms are caused by drain damage.

1937   Dr. Charles Bradley in Providence, Rhode Island, reports that a group of children with behavioral problems improved after being treated with Benzedrine, a stimulant medication.

1940s ADHD-like symptoms are thought to be caused by brain damage. The term *minimal brain damage* emerges.

1955 Ritalin (methylphenidate) is approved to treat minimal brain dysfunction by the U.S. Food and Drug Administration (FDA).

1957 The concepts and terms of *hyperkinetic behavior syndrome* and *hyperactive impulse disorder* are introduced.

1960 Dr. Stella Chess describes hyperactive child syndrome, a hyperactive condition that is not caused by brain damage.

1966 Samuel Clements formally defines *minimal brain dysfunction* as a combination of average or above-average intelligence with certain mild to severe learning or behavioral disabilities characterizing deviant functioning of the central nervous system.

1968 The *DSM-II* defines *hyperkinetic reaction of childhood* as a condition characterized by a short attention span, hyperactivity, and restlessness.

1980 The *DSM-III* defines *attention deficit disorder (ADD)* as a condition characterized primarily by a problem of inattention rather than of hyperactivity.

1987 The *DSM-III-R* (revised edition of the *DSM-III*), defines *attention deficit hyperactivity disorder (ADHD)* as a condition that includes both inattentive and hyperactive behaviors but does not differentiate between them.

1991 The U.S. Department of Education announces that students with ADHD will be protected under the Individuals with Disabilities Education Act.

1994 The *DSM-IV* recognizes two categories of ADHD—inattentive and hyperactive/impulsive—and three subtypes—primarily inattentive, primarily hyperactive/impulsive, and a combined type.

1996 Adderall gains approval from the FDA for the treatment of ADHD.

1999 New time-release delivery systems for ADHD medications are developed, eliminating the need for children with ADHD to have to take doses throughout the day. The results of the Multimodal Treatment Study of ADHD, one of the largest ADHD studies in history, are published in the *American Journal of Psychiatry*.

2000 Concerta (time-release methylphenidate) gains FDA approval for the treatment of ADHD.

2002 Strattera (atomoxetine) gains FDA approval for the treatment of ADHD.

2008 The American Heart Association issues recommendations that call for cardiovascular screening before prescribing stimulant treatment for all children diagnosed with ADHD. A report issued in the *Journal of American Psychiatry* finds conclusive evidence that stimulant treatment of young children with ADHD does not lead to later substance abuse.

ORGANIZATIONS TO CONTACT

The editors have compiled the following list of organizations concerned with the issues debated in this book. The descriptions are derived from the materials provided by the organizations. All have publications or information available for interested readers. The list was compiled on the date of publication of the present volume; the information provided here may change. Be aware that many organizations take several weeks or longer to respond to inquiries, so allow as much time as possible.

American Academy of Child and Adolescent Psychiatry (AACAP)
3615 Wisconsin Ave. NW, Washington, DC 20016-3007
(202) 966-7300
fax: (202) 966-2891
communications@aacap.org
www.aacap.org

AACAP is a nonprofit organization representing child and adolescent psychiatrists. The organization seeks to promote an understanding of mental illnesses, remove the stigma associated with them, advance efforts in prevention of mental illnesses, and assure proper treatment and access to services for children and adolescents. AACAP's *Journal of the American Academy of Child and Adolescent Psychiatry* focuses on psychiatric research and treatment of children.

American Psychiatric Association (APA)
1000 Wilson Blvd.
Ste. 1825
Arlington, VA 22209
(703) 907-7300
apa@psych.org
www.psych.org

The APA is a national medical specialty society representing psychiatrists. The mission of the APA is to promote quality care for individuals with mental disorders and their families, promote psychiatric education and research, advance and represent the profession of psychiatry, and serve the professional needs of its membership. The APA publishes several journals and newspapers, including the *American Journal of Psychiatry* and *Psychiatric News.*

Attention Deficit Disorder Association (ADDA)
PO Box 543
Pottstown, PA 19464
(484) 945-2101
fax: (610) 970-7520
mail@add.org
www.add.org

The ADDA is a nonprofit organization that seeks to provide information, resources, and networking to adults with ADHD and to the professionals who work with them. In doing so, the ADDA hopes to generate awareness, empowerment, and connections worldwide in the field of ADHD. The organization sponsors a national conference and produces audio- and video-tapes and teleclasses on ADHD topics. The association also publishes the journal *FOCUS* on a quarterly basis and an electronic newsletter.

Children and Adults with Attention-Deficit/Hyperactivity Disorder (CHADD)
8181 Professional Pl.
Ste. 150, Landover, MD 20785
(301) 306-7070 or (800) 233-4050
fax: (301) 306-7090
conference@chadd.org
www.chadd.org

CHADD is a national nonprofit organization providing education, advocacy, and support for individuals with ADHD. CHADD publishes a variety of materials providing information on current research advances, medications, and treatments affecting individuals with ADHD. These materials include *Attention!* magazine, the *CHADD Information and Resource Guide to ADHD, News from CHADD*, an electronically mailed current events newsletter, and other publications of specific interest to educators, professionals, and parents.

Federation of Families for Children's Mental Health (FFCMH)
9605 Medical Center Dr., Ste. 280
Rockville, MD
(240) 403-1901
fax: (240) 403-1909
ffcmh@ffcmh.org
www.ffcmh.org

The FFCMH is a national nonprofit organization dedicated to helping children with mental health needs and their families achieve a better quality of life. The organization advocates at the national level for children with mental health needs and provides leadership and assistance to local family-run child-serving organizations. The FFCMH publishes *Claiming Children,* several *Facts and Tips* publications, and several other books and guides about ADHD.

IDEA Partnership
1800 Diagonal Rd.
Ste. 320
Alexandria, VA 22314
(877) IDEA-info
www.ideapartnership
.org

The IDEA Partnership is dedicated to improving outcomes for students and youth with disabilities by joining state agencies and stakeholders through shared work and learning. The partnership facilitates interaction and shared work across professional and family organizations around common interests. Its Web site provides a section called "Many Voices," which provides citations and links to articles concerned with general and special education and other issues in Web-based journals and other periodicals.

National Center on Birth Defects and Developmental Disabilities (NCBDDD)
Centers for Disease Control and Prevention
1600 Clifton Rd.
Atlanta, GA 30333
(404) 639-3311
cdcinfo@cdc.gov
www.cdc.gov/ncbddd/
ADHD

NCBDDD promotes the health of babies, children, and adults, and it enhances the potential for full, productive living. The NCBDDD is a part of the U.S. Centers for Disease Control and Prevention, which is the main health agency of the U.S. government. The NCBDDD provides reports, statistics, and other information about ADHD.

National Dissemination Center for Children with Disabilities
PO Box 1492
Washington, DC 20013
(800) 695-0285
fax: (202) 884-8441
nichcy@aed.org
www.nichcy.org

The National Dissemination Center for Children with Disabilities, previously the National Information Center for Children and Youth with Disabilities, is part of Technical Assistance and Dissemination, which includes more than forty projects funded by the U.S. Department of Education's Office of Special Education and Rehabilitative Services. These projects offer information and technical assistance on a broad range of disability and special-education issues. The organization provides information about disabilities in children and youth; programs and services for infants, children, and youth with disabilities; the nation's special-education law; the No Child Left Behind law; and research-based information on effective practices for children with disabilities. The organization's Web site provides several publications about disabilities, including ADHD.

National Institute of Mental Health (NIMH)
Science Writing, Press, and Dissemination Branch
6001 Executive Blvd.
Rm. 8184 MSC 9663
Bethesda, MD
20892-9663
(866) 615-6464
fax: (301) 443-4279
nimhinfo@nih.gov
www.nimh.nih.gov

NIMH is the leading agency of the U.S. government concerned with mental health issues. The mission of the NIMH is to reduce the burden of mental illness and behavioral disorders through research on mind, brain, and behavior. The agency publishes various booklets, fact sheets, and easy-to-read materials on mental health issues.

Society for Neuroscience (SFN)
1121 Fourteenth St. NW, Ste. 1010
Washington, DC
20005
(202) 962-4000
fax: (202) 962-4941
info@sfn.org
www.sfn.org

The SFN works to provide professional development activities and educational resources for neuroscientists and to educate the public about the findings, applications, and potential of neuroscience research. The organization has several online publications, including *Brain Backgrounders*, an online series of articles that answer basic neuroscience questions, and *Brain Briefings*, a monthly two-page newsletter explaining how basic neuroscience discoveries lead to clinical applications.

Substance Abuse and Mental Health Services Administration (SAMHSA)
Center for Mental Health Services
1 Choke Cherry Rd.
Rockville, MD 20857
(240) 276-1310
fax: (240) 276-1320
shin@samhsa.hhs.gov
www.samhsa.gov

SAMHSA, part of the U.S. Department of Health and Human Services, seeks to ensure that people who suffer from mental health or substance abuse disorders have the opportunity to live fulfilling and meaningful lives. The agency's vision is expressed by the motto "A Life in the Community for Everyone." SAMHSA works to expand and enhance prevention and early intervention programs and improve the quality, availability, and range of mental health and substance abuse treatment and support services in local communities across the United States. The agency publishes a bimonthy newsletter, *SAMHSA News*, as well as various recurring statistical reports on mental health and substance abuse.

FOR FURTHER READING

Books

Lenard Adler and Mari Florence, *Scattered Minds: Hope and Help for Adults with Attention Deficit Hyperactivity Disorder.* New York: G.P. Putnam's Sons, 2006. This book provides information for adults with ADHD, such as the hidden warning signs of the disorder, new medications for treating it, and strategies for coping with it.

Susan Ashley, *The ADD & ADHD Answer Book.* Naperville, IL: Sourcebooks, 2005. Ashley poses questions and provides in-depth answers to numerous questions people may have about ADHD.

Russell Barkley, Kevin Murphy, and Mariellen Fischer, *ADHD in Adults: What the Science Says.* New York: Guilford, 2008. Barkley, a leading ADHD researcher, provides information and insight into adult ADHD, including answers to questions concerning such topics as the important differences between childhood and adult ADHD.

Peter Conrad, *The Medicalization of Society: On the Transformation of Human Conditions into Treatable Disorders.* Baltimore: Johns Hopkins University Press, 2007. Conrad discusses the consequences to society of thinking that every problem is medical in nature and requires treatment with medication.

Stephen Ray Flora, *Taking America Off Drugs: Why Behavioral Therapy Is More Effective for Treating ADHD, OCD, Depression, and Other Psychological Problems.* Albany: State University of New York Press, 2007. Flora maintains that Americans have been deceived into believing that whatever one's psychological problem, there is a drug to cure it. He argues that most psychological problems are behavioral, not chemical, and advocates behavioral therapy as an antidote.

Robert Jergen, *The Little Monster: Growing Up with ADHD.* Lanham, MD: Scarecrow Education, 2004. Jergen tells his own story of growing up with ADHD and the effects the disorder has had on him, his family, friends, coworkers, and lovers.

Jay Joseph, *The Missing Gene.* New York: Algora, 2005. Joseph finds serious flaws in the family, twin, and adoption studies generally used to support a genetic basis for attention deficit hyperactivity disorder, autism, and other disorders.

Kathleen G. Nadeau, *Survival Guide for College Students with ADHD.* Washington, DC: Magination, 2006. Nadeau, a clinical psychologist, provides advice to college and high school students with ADHD about how to succeed in college and life.

Benjamin Polis, *Only a Mother Could Love Him: My Life with and Triumph over ADD.* New York: Ballantine, 2004. Polis, diagnosed with ADHD at age eight, recalls his school days when he bullied classmates, downed a power line with a fishing spear on a family vacation, and was suspended for stunts like molding a face that resembled a penis in art class.

Adam Rafalovich, *Framing ADHD Children: A Critical Examination of the History, Discourse, and Everyday Experience of Attention Deficit/Hyperactivity Disorder.* Lanham, MD: Lexington, 2004. Rafalovich provides historical perspectives on ADHD along with the everyday accounts of ADHD from parents, teachers, clinicians, and ADHD children.

Peg Tyre, *The Trouble with Boys.* New York: Crown, 2008. Tyre discusses ADHD in the context of the national debate about why boys are falling behind girls in school achievement and are not attending college in the same numbers.

Timothy Wilens, *Straight Talk About Psychiatric Medications for Kids.* New York: Guilford, 2004. Wilens provides frank information for parents faced with making decisions about medicating their children.

Periodicals

Marilyn Elias, "Teen Girls with ADHD at Higher Risk of Mental Illness," *USA Today*, May 24, 2005.

Katie Engelhart, "Now, That's Using Your Noggin: Using Brain Waves to Fix ADD, Treat Seizures—and Move Light Sabres," *Maclean's*, September 3, 2007.

Stephen V. Faraone, "The Molecular Genetics of ADHD," *Psychiatric Times*, August 1, 2005.

Shellye Jofre, "What Next for Craig?" *Panorama: BBC News*, November 12, 2007.

Shawn Macomber, "Medication Is the Answer," *American Enterprise*, June 2005.

Diana Mahoney, "ADHD in Girls Linked to Mood, Eating Disorders," *Behavioral Pediatrics*, January 2008.

Melissa Marino, "Link Between Gene Variant, ADHD Identified," *Reporter: Vanderbilt Medical Center*, December 8, 2006.

Andres Martin, "Stimulating: Prescribing Amidst Controversy," *American Journal of Psychiatry*, April 2006.

Steven Nissen, "ADHD Drugs and Cardiovascular Risk," *New England Journal of Medicine*, April 6, 2006.

Fred Ottoboni, "Can Attention Deficit-Hyperactivity Disorder Result from Nutritional Deficiency?" *Journal of American Physicians and Surgeons*, Summer 2003.

Susan Smalley, "Reframing ADHD in the Genomic Era: The Emerging View of ADHD in the 21st Century: More Complex than Previously Believed," *Psychiatric Times*, June 2008.

Peg Tyre, "A Problem in the Brain; ADHD Medicine Is Not Just for Children Anymore," *Newsweek*, October 17, 2005.

Debra Viadero, "ADHD Experts Fear Brain-Growth Study Being Misconstrued," *Education Week*, December 5, 2007.

Internet Sources

John P. Barbuto, "ADHD: Disease or Social Misfit?" *Journal of Managed Care Pharmacy*, May 2005. www.amcp.org/data/jmcp/editorial_342-351.pdf.

Sam Goldstein, "Attention Deficit Hyperactivity Disorder (ADHD) in Adults," Attention Deficit Disorder Resources,

November 28, 2007. www.addresources.org/article_adhd_adult_goldstein.php.

Grace E. Jackson, "The Under Reported Story: ADHD, Stimulants, and the FDA," Psychrights.org, February 18, 2006. http://psychrights.org/articles/articles.htm.

Karin Klein, "Pencils, Pens, Meds," *Los Angeles Times*, August 20, 2007. www.latimes.com/news/opinion/la-oe-klein20aug20, 0,6706516.story?coll=la-opinion-center.

Christine B. Phillips, "Medicine Goes to School: Teachers as Sickness Brokers for ADHD, *PLoS Medicine*, April, 2006. http://medicine.plosjournals.org/perlserv/?request=get-document&doi=10.1371/journal.pmed.0030182.

Michelle Trudeau, "Adopted Teens Face Higher Risk for *ADHD*," *National Public Radio: Morning Edition*, May 6, 2008. www.npr.org/templates/story/story.php?storyID-90184184.

Momie Tullotes, "Is Lead Poisoning Causing Some Cases of LD, ADD & ADHD?" Associatedcontent.com, November 28, 2007. www.associatedcontent.com/article/457538/is_lead_poisoning_causing_some_cases.html?cat=25.

Judith Warner, "Ritalin Wars," *New York Times*, November 15, 2007. http://warner.blogs.nytimes.com/2007/11/15/ritalin-wars/.

INDEX

A

AAP Grand Rounds (journal), 101
Academic functioning, 82
Accidents, 81–82
Adderall, 9, 11, *111*
Adelizzi, Jane, 35, 40
ADHD gene, *49*
Adults/adulthood
  ADHD in, 26–32, *30*, 45
  untreated ADHD in, 82
Agency for Healthcare Research and Quality
  (AHRQ), 107
American Academy of Child and Adolescent
  Psychiatry, 21
American Academy of Pediatrics (AAP), 101
American Heart Association, 107, 109, 110,
  113–114
American Journal of Psychiatry, 32
American Medical Association (AMA), 78
American Psychological Association, 69
Antidepressants, 21–22
Archives of Pediatric and Adolescent Medicine
  (journal), 87
Attention deficit hyperactivity disorder
  (ADHD)
  in adults, 26–32, *30*, 82
  annual societal cost of, 68
  causes of, 18
  delayed brain growth and, 41–45
  diagnostic criteria, 19–20, 28, 61–63
  ethnic/racial differences in incidence of, 62
  gender differences in, *37*

  genes for, nomadic tribes and, 46–50, *47*
  girls and, 33–40
  heritability of, 48, 62
  intelligence quotient (IQ) and, *49*
  is a real medical disorder, 59–66, *61*
  is not a real medical disorder, 67–76
  is overdiagnosed, 89–97
  is underdiagnosed/undertreated, 77–88,
    87
  percent of children with, *22, 87*
  personal experience of, 127–133, 116–120,
    121–126
  positive aspects of, 120
  prevalence of, 17, 18, 60, 81, 103
  prognosis for, 24–25
  symptoms of, 16–17
  untreated, 81–83, *87*, 103–104
  See also Diagnosis; Medications; Treatment

B

Barkin, Ann, 116
Barkley, Russell, 73, 82, 119
Behavior modification therapy, 23, 85
Behavior rating scales, 71–72
Benson, Christena H., 103
Benson, D. Woodrow, 103
Biofeedback therapy, 101
Boyle, M., 73
Brain
  ADHD is related to delayed growth of,
    41–45
  growth of, *43*

Brain imaging techniques
facts about, *56*
may help diagnose/treat ADHD, 51–57
reveal abnormalities in neurological
pathways, 63

C
CAM. See Complementary and alternative
medicine
Canadian Medical Association Journal, 99
Centers for Disease Control and Prevention
(CDC), 38, 62, 113
Children and Adults with Attention Deficit/
Hyperactivity Disorder (CHADD), 75
Church of Scientology, 78
Circulation (journal), 105, 110
Clionsky, Mitchell, 38
Cognitive-behavioral therapy, 23
combined with medication, 31–32
Complementary and alternative medicine
(CAM)
may be useful in treating ADHD, 98–102
prevalence of use in children, *102*
Conduct disorder problems, 25
Council on Cardiovascular Disease in the
Young, 105
Crawford, Nicole, 33

D
Daily Pennsylvanian (college newspaper),
13
Davidson, Helen, 16
Death(s)
cardiac related, 110
in children/adolescents, *112*
*Diagnostic and Statistical Manual of Mental
Disorders (DSM)*, (American Psychological
Association), 19, 28, 69

Dietary therapy, 24, 100–101
Diller, Lawrence, 109
Dodson, William, 77
Driven to Distraction (Hallowell and Ratey),
26–27, 95

E
Education, of parents/patients, 65–66
EEG (electroencephalograph), *52*, 53, 54
EEG (electroencephalograph) biofeedback,
24
Emmond, Julie, 12
Environmental risk factors, 18, 65, 130
Equinox (college newspaper), 12

F
Faraone, Stephen V., 28, 59
Feingold, Ben, 18
Fish-oil supplements, 100
Food and Drug Administration, U.S. (FDA),
11, 99, 107
black box warning and, 96, 105
Ford-Martin, Paula Anne, 16

G
Ginko biloba, *100*
Ginseng, 100
Glaister, Tom, 89
Gonzalez, Angelica, 14
Guze, Samuel B., 61, 62

H
Hagberg, Laurie, 127
Hallowell, Edwin M., 26–27, 95
Herbal therapy, 24
Heritability, 48, 62
Hinshaw, Stephen P., 33, 34
Holistic therapy, 102

Homeopathic medicine, 24

I
Integrative Pediatrics Council, 102

J
Jensen, Jan, 55
Jensen, Lindsey, 55, 56
Jensen, Megan, 57
Jensen, Peter, 88
Jensen, Zach, 55–56, 57
Journal of American College Health, 80
Journal of Attention Disorders, 39
Journal of Clinical Psychology, 39
Journal of Consulting and Clinical Psychology, 34
Journal of Pediatric Psychology, 68
Journal of the American Medical Association, 99

K
Kapatkin, Jenn, 10

L
Lancet (journal), 95, 100
Littmann, Ellen, 36
Lowe, Sandlan, 55

M
Mahoney, Diana, 26
Maron, Barry, 107
Media, 60–61
Medications for ADHD
   adult views on, *96*
   adverse consequences of, 86–87, 96, 99
   are overprescribed, 89–97
   with behavioral therapy, 31–32
   children and heart screening and, 103-108,
   109–114
   emergency room visits related to, 101
   increase in cardiac symptoms from, *104*
   misuse of, 9–14, 80, 97
   side effects of, 11
Minnema, Lindsay, 41
Miranda, Fernando, 52, 53, 57
Multimodal Treatment Study of ADHD
   (MTA), 84–85, 88

N
Nadeau, Kathleen, 33–35, 36–38
Nalty, Ariane, 51
National Center for Gender Issues and
   ADHD (NCGI), 40
National Center for Health Statistics, 18,
   124, 131
National Comorbidity Survey Replication, 28
National Institutes of Mental Health
   (NIMH), 51, 53, 87
National Research Center on ADHD, 45
Neuropsychiatric disorders, ADHD as
   classic, 78–81
New York Times (newspaper), 13
Novartis, 95

O
Odle, Teresa G., 16

P
Parents
   ADHD and, 42, 85, 94–95
   are pressured to medicate children, 72–73,
   91
   education of, 65–66
Parker-Pope, Tara, 98
Pediatric Clinics of North America (journal),
   100

Peterson, Bradley, 54–55
Pharmaceutical companies, 74–75
Psychotherapy, 23

Q
Quinn, Patricia, 40

R
Radcliffe, Nick, 67
Ratey, John J., 26–27, 95
Reid, Robert, 72, 92
Research
    on ADHD treatment, 83–86
    on boys with ADHD, 35–36
    on girls with ADHD, 33–36
    on women with ADHD, 38–40
Ritalin (methylphenidate), 9, *10*, 68, 90
    as first-line treatment for ADHD, 70
    misuse of, 97
Robins, Eli, 61, 62
Rodgers, Danny, 52–53, 54, 57
Rodgers, Jeanne, 53
Rosen, Lawrence D., 102
Rostain, Anthony, 31
Rucklidge, Julia J., 36–37
Ryan, Fertman, 116

S
Safren, Steven A., 32
Saletan, William, 46
Schultz, David, 14
Self-medication, 27–28
Shipman, Claire, 51
Smalley, Susan, 48
Sogn, Richard, 11–12
St. John's wort, 99
Substance abuse, 25, 82
    of ADHD stimulants, 9–14, 80, 97

in adults with ADHD, 27, 35, 86–87
Substance Abuse and Mental Health Services
    Administration, 101
Sudden cardiac death (SCD)
    guidelines for screening for, 106–108
    incidence of in adults/children, 110
Surveys
    on abuse of ADHD drugs, 10–11
    on prevalence of ADHD medication, 68
    on use of CAM to treat ADHD, 102

T
Taking charge of ADHD (Barkley), 119
Taylor, Blake E.S., 121, *123*
Tics, 121–126
Timimi, Sami, 67
Tourette's syndrome, 124
Trappey, Ellen, 11
Treatment, 21–23
    alternative, 23–24
    most ADHD adults do not receive, 30–31
    research on optimal, 83–86
    See also Medications

V
Vetter, Victoria, 105, 107

W
Washington University Diagnostic Criteria,
    61–62
Weber, Wendy, 100
Women, with ADHD, difficulties for,
    38–40
World Health Organization (WHO), 28
World Mental Survey Initiative (WHO), 28

Y
Yale Daily News (college newspaper), 13